GHALIB
His Life and Poetry

Mirza Asadullah Khan Ghalib, who has been compared to Goethe by Iqbal is one of the most beloved and endearing of Urdu poets. Since his death a hundred years ago, countless editions of his poems have been published. Innumerable theses and treatises have been written on his work. Literary critics have been delighted with the versatility of his poetry which can be appreciated from so many angles.

In this little volume, the reader will get a glimpse of Ghalib's personality as well as his poetry. In the first section, Ali Sardar Jafri, one of the greatest litterateurs in Urdu, has given a brief biographical sketch of Ghalib and an appreciation of his personality and poetry. There follows translation of excerpts from Ghalib's letters. In the second section, some of the most beautiful couplets and ghazals of Ghalib from Urdu as well as Persian are rendered into English by the distinguished writer Qurratulain Hyder. This work is sponsored by Ghalib Yadgar Committee and its president, Dr Rafiq Zakaria, has contributed a foreword to this volume.

ALI SARDAR JAFRI — *Urdu poet and critic whose work has been translated into many foreign languages* — *winner of the Soviet Land Nehru Literary Award for his book of poems* Ek Khwab Aur; *Editor, Hindustani Book Trust, Bombay. He has edited and published works of many classical Urdu and Hindi poets, including Ghalib, Mir, Kabir and Mirabai. He was the recipient of the Jawaharlal Nehru Fellowship (1969-70) and worked on the imagery in Urdu poetry which was to be published in six volumes both in Hindi and Urdu. Unfortunately, this great man is no longer amidst us. He passed away in the year 2000.*

QURRATULAIN HYDER — *Urdu novelist and short story writer. Winner of the Sahitya Akademi Award for her book* Patjhar Ki Awaz. *She has been awarded the Soviet Land Nehru Award also for her translation of Sholokhov's story* The Fate of Man. *Her most celebrated novel is* Aag Ka Darya, *an epic spanning 5000 years of Indian history.*

Published by
Sterling Publishers Private Limited

GHALIB
His Life and Poetry

ALI SARDAR JAFRI
QURRATULAIN HYDER

Foreword by
RAFIQ ZAKARIA
President, Ghalib Yadgar Committee

A Sterling Paperback

STERLING PAPERBACKS
An imprint of
Sterling Publishers (P) Ltd.
A-59 Okhla Industrial Area, Phase-II,
New Delhi-110020.
Tel : 6916165, 6916209, 6912677, 6910050
E-mail: ghai@nde.vsnl.net.in
www.sterlingpublishers.com

Ghalib: His Life and Poetry
©2002, Ali Sardar Jafri and Qurratulain Hyder
ISBN 81 207 2167 5

All rights are reserved. No part of this publication may be reproduced, stored in a retrieval system or transmitted, in any form or by any means, mechanical, photocopying, recording or otherwise, without prior written permission of the original publisher.

Published by Sterling Publishers Pvt. Ltd., New Delhi-110016.
Lasertypeset by Vikas Compographics, New Delhi-110020.
Printed at : Shagun Offset Press, New Delhi-29

TO
LALA YODHRAJ

Foreword

Ghalib died in the same years that Gandhi was born and though there is little in common between the two—either in their intellectual approach or philosophical bend, both were, in their own way, great lovers of humanity possessing a catholicity of outlook and a breadth of understanding, which surpass the difference that, otherwise, separate them wide apart. Both were humanists to the core and rebels against narrowness and sectarianism; to them all mankind was one and its woes and sufferings a matter of the deepest concern.

That is why, like Gandhi, Ghalib will always remain a part of our national heritage. He was a poet who wrote in both Urdu and Persian; none before him composed Urdu poems as beautifully as he did; none after him. He was a magician with words. His poems are like the petals of a rose; their music is enchanting like a flute. But it is the delicacy and refinement of his thought, which are the sources of his greatness; they elevate us and touch the innermost recesses of both our head and our heart.

Mirza Asadullah Khan—to give the poet his full name—was born at Agra on December 27, 1797; Ghalib was his takhallus or poetic name. He began writing poetry, as a young boy of 12, and within seven years acquired such proficiency in it that his fame spread to different parts of India. He became a literary rage from Delhi to Calcutta. This was the time of the decline of the Mughal Empire; the resultant degeneration had corrupted every aspect of life. Despite Ghalib's greatness, he was side-tracked and lesser poets were preferred; he had to run from pillar to post to make a living; he was a failure in the only love affair that he had; his wife bore him children but they all died young; even his nephew, whom he adopted as his son, passed away in the prime of youth. As if these calamities were not enough he saw in the wake of the Sepoy Rebellion of 1857, the sack and destruction of his beloved city of Delhi, where he had settled down; he became a helpless witness of the murder of his own friends and relations. In deep anguish, he sang:

> I have known want and woe and fear;
> I have known this world to be a House of Pain,
> of sad bereavement and decay;
>
> I have known too father's grief for his dead sons;
> I have lived life but dreaded life itself;
> I have seen merit unrewarded go;
> I have seen golden garlands worn
> round parish donkey's necks;
> I have seen a royal charger gall his back
> with a pack pony's load;
>
> I have seen fools drink 'Sherbet'
> or rose-water and candy loaf;
> I have seen the wise suck their own heart's blood;
> I have seen a poet, a courtier at the court,
> strut peacock-like;

> I have seen a poet, beloved of the people beg for a pittance from the King;
>
> I have been a helpless witness of man killing man in civil strife and mutiny;
> I have watched an Empire falling to decay and dying;
> I have watched an Emperor taken captive and exiled to an alien land;
> I have felt old foundations shifting as on sand crashing.
>
> So have I lived and passed my days.
> How can I bring myself to say that God exists,
> God the Bounteous Giver, God the Beneficent?
> For God's possible for those who lead happy sheltered lives,
> And know God's grace and his loving care.*

And still these sufferings did not embitter Ghalib. He had the capacity to rise above them, and go in search of the truth of existence. His experiences only made him realise the limitations of his outlook. As he put it:

> Ask me not why I am sad,
> what grief both clutch my heart.
> My heart hath built me a prison-cell,
> and raised grim walls of narrow truths
> of cramping loves and hates.
> It shuts in the horizons of my thought,
> and clips my fancy's wings.*

Ghalib comes near to the realisation of truth, when drawing inspiration from Lord Krishna, he explains the cause of human unhappiness:

> Non-attachment is not indifference,
> or shrinking from the world of men,
> nor does renunciation justify,
> estrangement from our fellow-men.
> If thou dost dread life's fever-fret,
> or if to thee life seems to be
> a waste and wilderness,
>
> then shun thine ego; It is the source
> of thine unhappiness.
> Shun not thy fellow-men.*

But Ghalib was not a moralist; nor did he decry the temptations, to which man succumbed. He himself was no puritan and openly declared that but for his addiction to wine he might have even ended as a saint. But sainthood held no attraction for him for he was never enamoured of paradise and often said that it was nothing more than a pleasant thought to console the pious among the humans. On the contrary, Ghalib lived every moment of his existence on this earth and reacted to every situation with a rare sensitivity. To quote from one of his romantic poems:

> I would not mind thine angry looks,
> and could forgive thy teasing ways;
> thy wilful negligence;
> for we could hope to make it up,
> if thou wert angry for a while.

> But what I dread as prison is
> thy look of indifference.
> It tells me of thine unconcern
> and that I matter not to thee.*

At another place, Ghalib—sad and unhappy—reacts against pity or sympathy and asks those, who want to sympathise with him in his suffering, to leave him alone for he was a man and not a stone. As he puts it:

> Leave me, oh! Leave me alone,
> and let me weep.
> Why shall I not weep?
> I am not stock or stone;
> I am not wood.
> I have a tender heart
> moved by compassion and pain.*

A rare literary gem is Ghalib's Persian poem, *Charagh-i-Dair*, which has been translated so effectively by Miss Qurratulain Hyder, and reproduced, along with the translation of many other Urdu and Persian poems, in this book. Miss Hyder is proficient in both Urdu and English; she is, therefore, eminently readable and succeeds, to a great extent, in conveying the spirit of Ghalib to the readers.

Ali Sardar Jafri is one of the greatest litterateurs in Urdu. In poetry, he has few equals; there is depth in his compositions which is only matched by the beauty of his expressions. On Ghalib, he is an authority; his treatise, therefore, is a masterpiece and adorns the opening pages of this book.

I am happy that both these literary luminaries, who have enriched Urdu literature so much, responded to the request of the Ghalib Yadgar Committee to give such an excellent contribution; it is one of the finest works on Ghalib that has appeared in the English language.

Bombay

Rafiq Zakaria
President, Ghalib Yadgar Committee

---

* These English renderings of Ghalib's poems are by Prof J. L. Kaul, whose book, entitled *Interpretations of Ghalib*, with a foreword by the late Maulana Abul Kalam Azad is another successful effort at presenting Ghalib to the English readers.

Contents

Foreword *by Rafiq Zakaria*	vii
PART I: GHALIB *By Ali Sardar Jafri*	1
Ghalib	3
Excerpts from Ghalib's Letters *Translated from the Urdu by Qurratulain Hyder*	23
Introduction	25
PART II: HIS POETRY *Translated by Qurratulain Hyder*	65
Poems translated from Persian	69
The Ideal Men	71
A Persian Ghazal	74
To My Beloved	76
Charagh-i-Dair (Temple Lamps)	79
Abr-i-Guhar-Bar (The Pearl-Showering Cloud)	82
Poems translated from Urdu	85
Ghazal	87
Selected Couplets	89
Ghazal	99
Selected Couplets	100
Odes to Ali	106

Part I

GHALIB
by
Ali Sardar Jafri

Ghalib

Despite the boundless range of the human mind, individual intelligence has always had its limitations. The greatest of poets and thinkers cannot be an exception to this restrictive law of nature.

Nevertheless, when a creative mind alienates its image and places it before the world like a mirror in which the universe is reflected, the private vision acquires cosmic significance. Posterity interprets this vision in the context of its own thinking, perception and emotion, and finds new meanings in it with the passage of time. And thus a line from Shakespeare or a verse of Ghalib can be interpreted in a thousand different ways and situations. Great literature has the capacity to contain the future.

In literary criticism this capacity is known as universalisation, with its wealth of nuances and overtones. It distinguishes great literature from mere jugglery of words. Poetry acquires this quality when its creator, apart from being alive to his era, also bestows that special cadence and meaning to his words which strike the right chords. Ghalib is one of the very few poets to have reached this exacting standard of great poetry.

Mirza Asadullah Khan Ghalib, who has been compared to Goethe by Iqbal,* is one of the most beloved and endearing of Urdu poets. During the last hundred years countless editions of his *Diwan* (the collection of his poems) have been published. Innumerable theses and treatises have been written on his work. Literary critics have been delighted with the versatility of his poetry which can be appreciated from so many angles. Ghalib has received lavish tributes, his work has been seriously analysed, and at times he has been the subject of that exaggerated Oriental adoration which is, after all, a charming embellishment of art.

Ghalib's personality was many-sided and extremely attractive. Born at Agra, India, on 27th December, 1797, he was racially an Aibak Turk, his grandfather having migrated to India from Samark half a century earlier.

Of slender and well-proportioned physique, his face was oval, with sharp features and long and thick eyelashes. He had a fair and rosy complexion. His temperament was Iranian and he professed the Islamic faith. By culture and upbringing he was an Indian. His language was Urdu.

Ghalib was endowed with a rare intellect, transcendental vision and an outstanding and ingenious artistry. His genial nature and inherent courtesy overshadowed the egocentric traits of his character. Ghalib began writing poetry at a very early age. Before he was twenty-five he had already composed some of his finest *ghazals* (lyrics) and *qasidas* (odes). By the age of thirty-two he had become the literary rage from Delhi to Calcutta. Details of his education have not yet come to light, but we do know that Ghalib had full command of the branches of knowledge studied during his

---

* Dr (Sir) Mohammad Iqbal, the greatest modern Urdu poet (died 1938) of undivided India. Now, the national poet of Pakistan. His poems have been translated into English by Prof Reynold A. Nicholson and Prof Victor Kiernan.

time. He had a deep knowledge of Persian language and literature. His study of life was vast. He writes: "By the time I had reached the age of seventy, apart from the jostling crowds of commoners, a cavalcade of seventy thousand men of consequence had passed before my weary eyes. Therefore, I can call myself a fairly shrewd judge of human beings." His personal friends included kings and tavern-keepers, Muslim scholars and English officials, noblemen as well as ordinary people. He often commented wistfully on the gaieties and frivolities of his younger days when he heartily enjoyed drinking bouts, visited courtesans and gambled. But while still in his mid-twenties, he was suddenly disenchanted with this kind of life, and turned to mysticism.

Of an astonishingly catholic bent of mind, Ghalib did not differentiate between Hindus, Muslims, Christians and Jews. He never said his prayers, did not fast during the month of Ramzan, and continued his love for drinking to the end of his days. He called himself a sinner and had an implicit faith in God, in the Prophet and in the religion of Islam. His appetite for the good things of life was enormous. He hungered for knowledge and also yearned for social position and worldly status. He loved good food, good wine, good music and pretty faces. Whenever he was in possession of some of these things he fancied himself to be happier than kings.

Some events in Ghalib's troubled life stand out as important landmarks and had a deep influence on his mind and art. His orphaned childhood; his stay in Delhi; and a fairly long visit made to Calcutta. The erratic and capricious vagaries of his youth were reflected in his early obtuse poetry. Ghalib had lost his father at the age of five. He had been denied a proper upbringing and was required to launch out in life entirely under his own steam. In an unsheltered life of his kind, recklessness and a sense of adventure take the upper hand. Life's trials and tribulations thus became the only guide and preceptor. Mir,* on seeing Ghalib's early work remarked: "A good mentor would turn this lad into a fine poet, otherwise he may end up writing nonsense." Apart from Mulla Abdul Samad, the Iranian whose existence is not yet fully proved, Ghalib learned only in the school of life. Though his early, extremely ambiguous and involved poetry was ridiculed in Agra, the young Ghalib with characteristic swagger brushed aside all adverse criticism. After his marriage he left Agra and settled in Delhi. In the Mughal capital he met renowned scholars and master poets and could not ignore their opinions. Before he was twenty-five he found himself concentrating on sound balanced verse.

His journey to Calcutta in 1827 came as another turning point in his life. He went there to sort out the affairs of the pension given to him by the government of the East India Company for the military services rendered by his father and uncle. There was also a property matter to be settled. In Calcutta, Ghalib not only saw glimpses of the modern age, he also bitterly realised the failure of his own life. Ghalib had imbibed the last flowering of Mughal culture. He was now greatly affected by the industrial civilisation introduced by the conquering British. But the greatest single factor to influence his life was perpetual destitution. This kept him in anguish to the very last day of his life.

The worldly glories of Ghalib's ancestors (who proudly traced their descent from the ancient kings of Iran) had departed long ago. The academic traditions of Avicenna had also vanished in preceding centuries. Therefore, Ghalib turned his pen into his personal heraldic banner. "The broken spears of the ancestors were transferred into a fiery

---
* Mir Taqi Mir, (1722—1810) one of the greatest Urdu poets.

quill." His pen illumined the wasteland of his life. His courageous spirit led him by still waters and green pastures. This magnificent sweep of his creativeness enriched Urdu literature for all time.

The important question now arises whether Ghalib possessed a world-view and a philosophy of life. He is certainly not the founder of a new school of thought, and it would be futile to look for an integrated or disciplined point of view or a message in his poetry. But the philosophical content and the high seriousness of his work cannot be overlooked. Despite the poetic contradictions created by the *ghazal's* conventional theme and imagery, a philosophical preoccupation with man and his universe remains dominant in his verse.

Ghalib was deeply influenced by medieval mystic traditions which, apart from his own studies, he had inherited from Persian and Urdu poetry. He once said, "Mysticism does not behove a poet." And yet he sought the help of sufi thought to understand life and to avoid the hypocrisies of formal religion. Mysticism also disciplined his unfettered and unconventional nature.

Ghalib believed in pantheism. In a Persian *masnavi* (narrative poem), he calls the cosmos, "the mirror of knowing whose reflections of the External Beauty fascinate the inner eye of the beholder. Wherever man turns his face he finds Him, and whichever side man turns is His own side."

In one of his prose writings in Persian he says, "The existence of an atom is naught beyond its I-ness. All emanates from Truth. The river flows everywhere, its waves and whirlpools rise on the surface. Everything is God."

Since existence is Unity and the Absolute is everlasting, the universe cannot be transient. Ghalib has not explicitly expressed this view anywhere, but in his Persian work *Mehri - Nimroze* (Midday Sun) he expresses the belief that the world has no exterior existence. Divine Being is the only Reality, the attributes are also Reality; the idea of independent existence of attributes is merely an illusion and a dream. "Though one may say it is, it is not." And so the question of permanence and transience, of renewal and decay does not arise. God's attributes or manifestations in the form of matter are identical with His Reality and Absolute Being, just as the rays of the sun are not exterior to the sun itself. A new Adam shall be born on the Day of Reckoning; Adam shall follow Adam and the world shall continue for evermore. (Hindu cyclic concept of time.)

This gives rise to a second query. If the world is a reflection of the Absolute, what, then is the origin of evil? Whence comes sorrow, pain and affliction? How can the contradictions be explained? The traditional reply to the query is that the reflection collects dross and is polluted as it moves away from the source. But the weakness of this logic is self-evident, for the distance of the reflection becomes a thing separate from the Absolute, and thus negates the view that all is God.

Ghalib raised this question but could not arrive at a satisfactory conclusion. This is reasonable. A poet should not be expected to solve an enigma which has baffled great mystics and philosophers of all ages. However, in the opening hymn of his Persian *masnavi* he could say, "The contradictions arise at a certain point of Ultimate Perfection." But this attractive turn of phrase is merely an elucidation of the doctrine of pantheism, and does not answer the fundamental question. A more poetic and reasonable answer is found in the first Persian ode in which Ghalib addresses God in these words:

Expressing thyself as non-self has caused chaotic discord.
Thou uttereth the Word and is lost in its illusion.

This distinction between God and His world, the duality between the creator and the creation, between self and non-self is such that the beholder and the object appear to be two separate entities despite being one and the same. "They are separated by the curtain of customary worship although unity cannot contain duality." Later, the poet reveals certain esoteric secrets and says, "Pain and sorrow emerge from the source, so that the pleasure of experiencing happiness may increase .... Trials and tribulations distinguish friend from foe. Life welcomes its tired guests on a carpet of thorns. They enjoy the comforts when they have overcome their weariness." The distinction between self and non-self results in a paradox which makes life what it is. This is the essence of non-duality. On this point, evil becomes a part of good and the difference between perfect and imperfect comes to an end. Spirit and matter, life and death are equated, and the belief of formal religion appears like a mirage. The act of rejecting the barriers of race and religion turns into an integral part of true faith that unites all humanity. The difference between joy and sorrow becomes meaningless, and spring and autumn are attuned to each other.

In one of his verses Ghalib employs the colourful imagery of the tavern ..... A prismatic wine-glass is forever in circulation, the seasons of decay and renewal being its different colours. Night and day are chasing one another ... a whirling movement of divine ecstacy, a swiftly revolving point in its frenzied flight turns itself into a dancing flame. Beyond the concepts of pleasure and pain, life is the exuberant, dynamic manifestation of the non-duality of all existence ... "The drowning man was slapped by the wave. The thirsty quelled his thirst at the river's bank. The river neither wished to drown one, nor did it wish to slake the thirst of the other." The river is absorbed in itself. Action and reaction are its waves which turn the present time into the future time and also the future time into the present time.

This pantheistic vision of Ghalib embraces the Vedanta as well as the neo-Platonic philosophy. His philosophy of the Absolute includes renunciation and negation of attributes. At the same time he adorns the person of the Qualified Absolute with gorgeous similes. In Ghalib's poetry we find a fascinating harmony of Persian and Tartar paganism and Hedonistic sensuousness. It depends on one's strength and capacity either to renounce worldly life on reaching a certain stage in one's spiritual evolution, or to pick up this colourful, musical toy called the world of senses.

Ghalib has certainly assumed an optimistic attitude through this belief and this optimism becomes the life-blood of his poetry. Sorrow is the basis of all joy. To avoid sorrow is to deny life. Playing with sorrow gives true meaning to existence. Death itself enhances the joy of living and bestows the courage to enjoy action. Man needs his various baptisms of fire which life amply provides. In his Persian *qasida* he says, "If the fire is strong I fan it more. I fight with death. I hurl myself on unsheathed swords. I play with daggers and shower kisses on arrows."

This defiance and courage makes Ghalib's melancholy a thing of enchantment. This glorious ecstasy of pain is not to be found in any other poet of Urdu. Iqbal is closer to Ghalib in this respect but the philosophical aspect of his poetry overshadows his zest for life.

It is impossible to separate the concord of joy and sorrow in Ghalib's poems. Therefore, it would be wrong to call him the poet of melancholy or the singer of joy. Ghalib sings of the joyous splendour of agony.

After this brief survey of his philosophy of life, it is not difficult to understand the place of man in Ghalib's universe. Man too, like other creatures, is a reflection of the Absolute. But he differs from other beings because of his capacity to think and distinguish between the right and the wrong. Man's conscience is a tempest of agitation and turmoil, "just as the water in life's ocean has its quality of wetness and silk within the cocoon that contains its silkiness." Moreover, man possesses reason and intellect. "His hands and mind combine together to create his character." His spirit and intelligence give him the power of expression. His mind, though limited, is yet a part of the Infinite Supreme Intelligence. In his *Mughanni Nama (The Singer and the Song)* Ghalib calls human wisdom "the decorator of the dawn-light of the mystics and the lamp that illumined the marble halls of the world, the dawn-light of the mystics and the lamp that illumined the ancient Greeks." The wondrous spectacle and the gaiety of the world is primarily due to man and his endeavours. Man is the very pivot of a universe which was solely created for him ….. "Round the point of my being revolves the compass of seven spheres."

This troublesome, energetic, zealous creature, made of humble clay, nevertheless, attempts to understand what it is all about.

He wants to remain an inquisitive spectator at all times and in all conditions. In order to reach the heart of mysteries he sometimes goes through fiery ordeals. If he cannot comprehend the content, he contemplates the form and ultimately reaches the beatific vision. As long as one possesses the wealth of imagination, fancy and desire, one arrives at the goal … "Whatever the coffer of life contains, is mine."

The traditional theme of renunciation has no place in Ghalib's poetry. As a gloriously happy pagan and an

Epicurean aesthete, Ghalib wishes to imbibe beauty with such intensity that his eyes are a barrier between himself and the object of his desire. Mere sight does not suffice and his heart longs for fulfilment. Sight disturbs oneness by keeping the illusion of duality alive. He drinks straight from the wine-pitcher. When he starts sinning "the river of ingenuity dries up in no time." He wants to change the very laws of pre-determination and free-will through the circulation of the wine-cup. He thinks *absurd* zest is as important as rebellious fortitude, to achieve one's ambitions. And this carries him to the stage of a refined and delightful sensuality. Perhaps his libertine and rakish youth had taught him that a reckless life may lead to ruin but it also sharpened one's mind and bestowed maturity.

The measures Ghalib creates for assessing his sensuality are in terms of his uncommitted and unfulfilled desires. With his tears he fathoms his defeats and failures. The entire wilderness cannot measure his fatigue. For, "when desert after desert overflows with his weariness," his "footsteps begin floating like bubbles on the sandy waves of his frenzied trail." The known world cannot satisfy his urge, "The Sahara of possibilities" is merely "a step in his eternal search." His poetry is a heady quest for the next step, a quest which is characterised by constant restiveness, pain, heart-burn and a movement like a river overflowing its banks.

Relish is his favourite word, along with *desire* and yearning. Madness, which is the last stage of longing, always spurs him on to greater madness. This dizziness which is the outcome of zest, "keeps a man aloft even when he is in the depth of abject misery." It gives "a speck of sand the immensity of a desert and turns a drop into a stormy river." He remains unsatisfied throughout his magnificent pursuit. For him journeying has greater pleasure than arrival. "When

I visualise Paradise and consider that if my sins are forgiven I'll be granted a Pearly Place together with a Houri, I find the thought depressing. To live with one single Houri till all eternity is an alarming thought indeed. Wouldn't that poor paragon of virtues get on my nerves? Imagine having only one emerald castle, under a solitary bough of Paradise ..." (in a letter).

Ghalib's early life had taught him to taste a little sugar but never to settle on honey like a bee... else the power of flight would be sapped. And so he became the poet of the uphill trek, not of destination, of non-fulfillment rather than consummation. The urge of the unattainable introduces one to the pleasure of lonely highways. This has enriched his poetry with a sense of movement, a concept expressed through a fusion of such images as the waves, storm, flame, mercury, lightning and flight. Movement has become a part of Ghalib's aesthetics. His beloved in his poetry is also swift and mercurial like flame and lightning. These highly dynamic word-pictures are the perfection of imagist poetry. The printed word dances under the spell of his novel metaphors and similes. Characters become fluid; abstract thought turns into a figure of life and colour. Arid wastelands steam up under the frenzy of his wanderings. The wilderness begins to run ahead of the wayfarer. Unsculptured idols begin to dance within the heart of the stone. Mirrors dissolve into eyes. The lines of the palm become throbbing veins in the hand of the cup-bearing saqi. Cypresses follow the beloved like her shadow. Attracted by the perfect height of the fair one, the boughs languidly yawn, rise and carry the flowers to her headdress. Time ambles on the road of restlessness. Years are not measured by the orbit of the sun, but by the flash of lightning. The true visionary sees the road ahead not as a mere track but as the throbbing vein of life.

Ghalib's poetic fancy is entirely an expression of his inner restiveness. He leaves much unsaid. This makes a poem difficult but more beautiful and profound.

Ghalib has turned his gay melancholy and hopeful agony into an imagery of dancing movement as a result of his own temperament and the healthier traditions of mystical poetry.

While analysing his emotional and psychological make-up, the background of the poet's social environment cannot be ignored. When Ghalib says that it is sinful to breathe outside 'the company of dreams' he does not reveal a longing for mundane riches and a few kisses. It is his desire for 'the garden yet uncreated,' whose ecstatic vision has compelled him to sing. To think that this is his subjective dream is to belittle his greatness as a visionary. The 'still uncreated garden' is an indication of his social awareness, for, this 19th century Urdu poet did possess a reasonably sound concept of social evolution and progress.

It is difficult to propound the real meaning of a *ghazal* because the motif is usually hidden in an intricately wrought facade of stereotyped imagery. Still a poet who called the world 'the mirror of knowing' could not be oblivious of his environment and remain content with the subjective romanticism of his 'bleeding heart'.

In his letters after 1857, he wrote painful elegies of the destruction of Delhi, often quoting his own verse and suddenly revealing the social content of his poetry.

Long before 1857 he had realised that the flickering candles of Mughal culture and society were about to blow out for ever. Although he greatly loved the values of his own ancient civilisation, yet he knew that its superstructure was fast decaying. The foundation had shaken and the roots had become rotten, ready to crumble before a gust of wind. His own life resembled the falling ruins of his culture. His personal melancholy was attuned to this collective melancholy pervading Delhi and Agra, and had saddened and disillusioned him in his youth. At the same time, as has been pointed out earlier, he had seen a glimpse of the new order based on scientific and industrial progress. He could not grasp the significance and the extent of the new economic exploitation of the country by a Western colonial power (if he did, we do not find its proof in any of his works). Nevertheless, he was greatly impressed by the science and industry introduced by the British. Many years before the Mutiny of 1857, Sir Syed Ahmad Khan* annotated Abul Fazl's *Ain-i-Akbari* and asked Mirza Ghalib to write a commentary on his historic work. The poet waived his old-world courtesy and frankly told the young scholar:

"Look at the Sahibs of England..... They have gone far ahead of our oriental forebears. Wind and wave they have rendered useless. They are sailing their ships under fire and steam. They are creating music without the help of the *mizrab* (plucker). Their magic words fly through the air like birds. Air has been set on fire..... Cities are being lighted without oil-lamps. This new law makes all other laws obsolete. Why must you pick up straws out of old, time-swept barns while a treasure-trove of pearls lies at your feet?"

The conclusion drawn by Ghalib is significant: the worth of *Ain-i-Akbari* can certainly not be doubted. But God is ever bountiful. Since goodness knows no end, good things become better and the betterment of the world continues from epoch to epoch. Therefore worshipping the dead in this way cannot be called a sound habit of mind. (Persian *masnavi* 10.)

---

* Muslim educationist and social reformer, founder of Muslim University, Aligarh, India.

Ghalib with his social consciousness preferred modern industrial order to the laws and decrees of Akbar's period and was in favour of giving scientific inventions and concepts an honoured place in poetry. (Letters) It was difficult for him to understand the economic relationships of the new social set-up. He did not know the inherent destructiveness of the new socio-economic structure. Still one of his couplets is astonishing in this context:

> Beauty and innocence are ravished by what else brings
>
> virgin rose-buds from the garden to the market place.

Ghazal is the epitome of subjective, lyrical poetry. Therefore it is hard to draw a line of demarcation between personal emotions and expressions of social discontent and protest. Still, it is easy to ascertain that Ghalib was not most dejected about his own times. This despair, born out of his personal misfortunes and historical events, becomes strangely moving in his verses. His life was extraordinarily tragic. As we have seen already; he lost his father at the age of five. Another calamity was the death of his uncle three years later. He spent his childhood with his widowed mother's prosperous but unsympathetic family. After a brief spell of youthful dissipation, his life remained a series of heart-breaks and disasters. From the age of nineteen he had to fight his own battles. He had no income of his own and his inherited property had been squandered away by others. In his constant and mostly unsuccessful attempts to obtain monetary support, Ghalib spent the rest of his life carrying petitions, writings *qasidas*, going from pillar to post in Delhi, Agra and Calcutta. He had to go through the soul-killing experience of writing empty and false odes eulogising the undeserving and worthless rich, and haughty English officials. Yet he continued drinking on borrowed money, living on friends' charity. At the time of his death in Delhi on

15 February 1869, he bitterly realised that his widow would be utterly destitute. He often hid himself within his house fearing legal summons, court bailiffs and creditors. Because of a plot instigated by his enemies, he also faced the disgrace of imprisonment on charges of gambling. The once-glorious Mughal court did not extend to him the patronage accorded to lesser poets. Towards the end of his life he was subjected to obscene abuses during the long-drawn out process of an academic controversy. In his younger days, the woman he loved died and her memory lived with him till the end of his life. His children died young. The nephew he had adopted as his son died in the prime of his youth. In 1857, Ghalib witnessed the sack and destruction of Delhi. He saw his dear friends murdered during the holocaust. Contemporary scholars were either hanged on the gallows as rebels or deported for life to distant Andaman Islands. Nothing was left for Ghalib but a dirge for the city that once was.

It pained him that the qualities of broad-mindedness, self-sacrifice and generosity were not appreciated. "It is not possible for the whole world to be well-fed and prosperous. But at least in the town where I lived, I wished that no one went hungry nor wore rags. Condemned by God and man, old, weak, ill, poverty stricken, I, who cannot bear to see others begging from door to door, must myself beg... that is I..." (in a letter).

This, then, is Ghalib's picture of man, for whom he weeps and can do nothing.

In another work he says, "God merely kindled the flame of faith. Man embellishes cities and lights up civilisations. He cried out to God complaining of injustices. But his grief for human suffering turned into sharp satire when he took up his own weapon. He raised his anguish from the level of emotion to the plane of intellect.

Ghalib laughed in the face of extreme hardships. His countless jokes and humorous anecdotes and most of all his letters tell us how bravely and cheerfully he faced hunger, disgrace and finally, death. A satirist becomes bitter when he has suffered intensely. His personal pride makes his slings poisonous, although superficially his light-hearted vein may appear to be mere joviality. Ghalib used his pungent wit as an armour against a very cruel world. His subtle irony and banter was mingled with his tears. His sharp satire also enabled him to laughingly receive his wounds. This ability to laugh contained the secret of his pride and individuality which an unkind world had turned into ego and conceit.

Ghalib's ego was a shield without which the world could not be confronted. He did not bow before his fellow beings, and did not give into romantic gloom, self-pity or world-weariness. He was not enamoured of Majnun or Farhad, the legendary tragic lovers, nor was he impressed by Alexander the conquerer or Khizr, the prophet who guided lost travellers. He was not interested in unfaithful beloveds. Even in his obedience to God, Ghalib remained as free and as self-contemplating as he was while adoring God's fickle creatures. He retained the same personal dignity in his *odes* (*quasidas*) though they are the weakest aspect of his creative life and art. Compelled by circumstances, he begged favours of the mighty. At the same time he remained miserably conscious of this degrading servility. ("I hate myself more than those who hate me.") In his preface to his Persian poems he regrets that half his life has been wasted praising fools. For this reason the purely adulatory parts of the odes are the weakest while the poetic prologues are always powerful. Ghalib was keenly aware of his own superiority to the subject of his ode and often slyly found a way to put in a few, oblique words in his own indirect praise.

Ghalib's last refuge was his own imagination and inspiration, for, "the poor depend for their life on their imagination." (Letters.) In the world of fancy a pauper can rule the world and make up for the wants of his actual life. No temporal king, only the maker of dreams can reign in these fantasy-realms where "potentates appear in the form of jaguars," and "poets become prophets." Gabriel sings here as the camel-driver of the Muse's caravan. In this world of dreams, cruelty is replaced by kindness, regrets give way to the joy of success. The drinker moulds his own exquisite wine-cup and creates his own special saqi. The river itself comes to the thirsty. Adversity engenders the determination to live. Bitter pills of sorrow create their own glow on the sufferer's face. Imagination goes flower-picking in virgin arbours and pours forth rhapsodies of spring. This fantasy-land, again, has vibrance, rhythm and airiness. "So that I have naught to do with Echoes."

This spiritual fortitude gives a new dimension to the idea of love, a dimension hitherto unknown in Urdu poetry. In the face of utterly un-Platonic, devastating, down-to-earth physical attraction despite his desperate surrender, Ghalib remains haughty and dignified as ever. He believes that a repressed sigh would turn into a painful heart-burn. Therefore "patience and restrain should be replaced by passionate anger." "If the beloved does not yield to one's pleas, she should be faced belligerently." The symbolism in *ghazals* imply that not only the beloved, but any ideal, even the desire for a better life, should be taken up like a challenge. Perhaps for this reason Ghalib calls himself "a rebel, irreverent to the polite rules of *ghazal*-writing."

This non-conformist poet appeared on the literary scene as a novel and unique personality, whose fiery assertion of self was tinged with a strange rebellion which expressed itself through scepticism, satire and romantic fancy. Ghalib's contemporaries could not understand this new mood which made the poet laugh through his tears and which gave a new grandeur and meaning to the human condition. None before Ghalib had poked fun at God and satirised the sacrosanct beloved with such haughty impatience. No other poet had turned "the sword of injustice into a sweeping wave" of his own "inner torment." No one before him had added such deep philosophical import to the sentiments of *ghazal*. Ghalib removed the difference between the language of *ghazal* and *qasida* and paved the way for modern Urdu poetry (Nazm).

Ghalib's popularity in the late 19th and early 20th century was mainly due to the fact that apart from other qualities, his poetic mood and temper was of a modern man. This new emotion is also in harmony with the mood and character of a new, emergent India which is proud of its past splendours, is sorrowful of its present and is seeking greater glories for tomorrow.

Ghalib did not write political poetry, but he represented the spirit of the modern age. And so, when Indian freedom fighters, visionaries and new poets came to the fore, they derived their inspiration and strength from him.

It is not accidental that Hali[*], who protested against the conventional and stylised Urdu poetry, was a disciple of Ghalib. Sir Syed, the educationist had heard Ghalib praise the new technological civilisation long before 1857 which is the great watershed of Indian history. Similarly, Maulana Shibli's[+] patriotic poems have echoes from Ghalib. Iqbal's philosophy and art bear an imprint of the great master. The

---
[*] Khwaja Altaf Hussain Hali (1837-1910), great Indian reformer, scholar, and poet.
[+] Poet, scholar and historian.

Urdu poets of succeeding generations including the modern and the very modern, have all been influenced by Ghalib in varying degrees, and tones. Countless lines from 'Uncle Ghalib', as he is affectionately called, have become proverbs in Northern India. Hardly an Urdu-speaking household is without its copy of the immortal *Diwan*. After Independence, Ghalib has become a bestseller in Hindi.

Today Ghalib's poetry has come down to us as an interpreter of the past as well as a pointer to the present. It possesses the pleasing hangover of a bygone era and the exhilarating intoxication of present times. It conveys to us the agony of the night that has fled and the joyful light of the sun that has newly risen.

Ghalib's greatness lies in the fact that he not only encompassed the inner turmoil of his age, he also created new urges, inner agitations and demands. Breaking through the bonds of time, his poetry reaches out into the past and the future. To use the language of the Oriental metaphor, Ghalib tested his personal experiences, born out of an exceedingly refined aesthetic sense, on the touchstone of human psychology and translated them into pure poetry. This gave him a universal voice, making him a poet who celebrated each individual moment of human life. He knew the varied states of the human soul. Extreme happiness or despair, conditions of religious doubt or miracle-making faith, profound metaphysics or utter trivialities, sensations of love-making and the pleasure of loving and being loved... Ghalib's poetry accompanies the reader through all stages of human experience. Lesser poets can adopt one of his attitudes as their personal philosophy, but Ghalib captivates us with his overpowering, comprehensive, larger than life genius.

To enjoy his poems, it is not enough to know superficial meanings. When read again and again, the words emerge as kaleidoscopic pictures. They become familiar like human faces and gradually reveal their personalities. The inner rhythm of their meanings emerges after the ears have got used to their outer music. Then from meaning of words you reach their poetic significance. You enter a world where *fidelity* is perfumed like the beloved's hair; where candle-lit cypresses dance, where love is a state of the human soul, an exquisite, passion filled action, a majestic deed and an aesthetic taste. In this special domain of Ghalib the loved one's beauty merges into the loveliness of the world at large, and the grandeur of the scimitar and the allure of charmers is dramatic and electric. As you continue to read, the pangs of separation would turn into rapturous, gladsome longing, and union with the beloved would be like the bliss of unfulfilled desire. Zest for life would appear as the all-powerful urge of creation. Madness would turn into a quest that is obstructed by prison chains and the high walls of the temple and the Kaaba. The reader would then see that these walls are decorated by utter weariness of the seeker.

Then, Ghalib's tavern would emerge before the readers' eyes as the destination of perfect humanism and complete freedom. And it is then that the pages of the *Diwan* would light up with Ghalib's thrilling creatures of imagination. His beloved would smile through the words and the world would become more beautiful and man would command greater respect.

Excerpts from Ghalib's Letters
Translated from Urdu by
Qurratulain Hyder

Introduction

Urdu prose came into its own at the turn of the 19th century when sagas, romances, fables and works on serious subjects began to be written in Calcutta, Delhi and Lucknow. Patterned after a formal Persian prose then prevalent in India, these early writings, with some exceptions, were highly florid and ornate. (They even had rhymed sentences!) Correspondence in Urdu was also as stylised and courtly. But, anyway, most business and personal letters were written in Persian, as writing in Urdu prose was still considered rather non-U.

Ghalib's letters serve as a landmark, for he introduced a natural, conversational style in prose. Writing to a friend, Mirza Hatim Ali Beg 'Mehr,' he says;

"Mirza Sahib, I have invented a style through which correspondence has become conversation. From a distance of a thousand miles you can speak through your pen, and enjoy company despite separation."

Dramatically, he often breaks into an imaginary dialogue with his correspondent or with some other character:

"Miran Sahib, *Assalam-o-Aleikum.*"

"Hazrat, *Adab.*"

"Say, Sahib, do I have leave to write to Mir Mehdi?"

"Huzoor, have I ever asked you not to?"

In a letter from Rampur to Mir Mehdi:

"Aha, ha, ha, my dear, dear Mir Mehdi has arrived. Come along, Bhai, do take a seat. How are you? This is Rampur, the abode of joy…

Informing his relative, Nawab Alai, about the departure of the womenfolk for Loharu:

" I am sitting near the porch. Mohammed Beg (servant) passes by.

I say, Mian Mohammed Beg, have the ladies left for Loharu?

Not yet, Hazrat.

Don't they, by any chance intend leaving?

They do, Sire, they do. They are almost ready, Sire."

Ghalib's letters are spontaneous and gay, witty and philosophical, reflecting the many facets of the poet's warm personality. Picturesquely they reveal his follies and weaknesses, his erudition and scholarship, as well as his tremendous sense of humour. Disarmingly honest, he sometimes swears and uses bad language when angry. With relish he describes the menus for his lunch and dinner, his joy at receiving a basket of fresh mangoes or a bottle of Old Tom, his apparel at the time of writing, his household, his silly maidservant, the seasons. Delhi, which like Shakespeare's and Dr Johnson's London was renowned for its scholars, writers and poets, suddenly comes to an end in 1857. With a novelist's keen eye for detail and with a poet's sensibility he poignantly depicts his turbulent and heartbreaking times.

The poet wrote several hundred letters to a surprisingly large number of friends, admirers, disciples, as well as relatives and patrons. His correspondents belonged to a cross-section of society including potentates and penniless bards.

The first collection of Ghalib's letters entitled *Ood-i-Hindi* (The Incense of India) appeared four months before his death, from Meerut. The second, *Urdua-i-Mualla* (Sublime Urdu), Vol. I was published from Delhi after the poet died; Vol. II was brought out by Khwaja Altaf Hussain Hali in 1899. Other anthologies of Ghalib's Urdu and Persian correspondence dealing with literary problems and controversies have also been published.

Ghalib's letters are invaluable not only to the social historian but also to the student of elegant and idiomatic, standard Urdu. The translation obviously cannot convey either the subtlety and finesse or the vigorous flow and lucidity of the language which, because of these very characteristics, is most difficult to render into another, especially a Western language.

Passages in which Ghalib discusses literature, prosody, linguistics, history, etc., have been omitted from the following brief extracts arranged in chronological order.

Q. H.

To Munshi Har Gopal 'Tufta'*

Maharaj, your kind letter. Although I am worthless and the lowliest of human beings, consider me your well-wisher. What can I do? I cannot be a *bhat* in my odes. You'll notice that my odes have more of poetic thought and less of eulogy; the same is true of my prose...

May 1848.

To Har Gopal 'Tufta'

...You know Nawab Zainudulbedin Khan Arif's⁺ sons have come to stay with me. You are like my son too. Therefore your *ghazals* are my grandchildren. Arif's children don't let me eat, jump on my cot with bare feet, spill water, raise dust all over the house and I don't mind. How would I mind my metaphorical grandchildren who are not even naughty?

June 18, 1852.

To Har Gopal 'Tufta'

Your letter yesterday; learned about your problem.⁺⁺ When I advice a friend I say to my own heart: Put thyself in this man's place and think how thou wouldn't have behaved if thou had been afflicted thus..... How can I tell you to bear your dishonour and not give up the friendship..... In any case one must always remain loyal to one's friend and overlook his deeds... The Jaipur affair is incidental.⁺⁺⁺ I had hoped for

---

* A Persian and Urdu poet of Sikanderabad, Bulandshehr (UP), Tufta was one of Ghalib's closest friends and 'Shagirds' or disciples in poetry. Ghalib sent him the largest number of letters—one hundred and twenty-three-over the year.

+ Begum Ghalib's young nephew who died in April, 1852. His children were adopted by the poet.

+ Perhaps Tufta and Jani Bankey Lal 'Rind' (another disciple of Ghalib), had, had a quarrel and Tufta wanted to give up his job.

+++ Ghalib wanted to send his *Diwan* to the Maharaja of Jaipur.

some benefit. Growing old and deaf, I have also acquired a bad reputation and a blot on my name.++ Can't get a position in any state except as a mentor or an ode-writer, so that I could get something for myself or promote a friend.

December 10, 1852.

To 'Tufta'

Bhai... I am greatly worried. It is rumoured that the Raja of Bharatpur has died. I am worried about Janiji and for you, since you are also in the same territory. The English have introduced a law according to which after the death of the ruler the Government takes over the administration of his State till such time as the heir attains majority. During this interim period old employees are not dismissed. As such Janiji's position remains secure, but he is the Vakil and I don't know how his relations are with the Mukhtar and the Rani. Janiji had attached you with this state, and you led a prosperous and gay life. Please do not remain so carefree now. I heard about it late evening and was so perturbed that I didn't go to the Fort this morning. Am sending this letter unstamped so that it reaches you safely. Half an anna is nothing but the Dak people treat unstamped letters as urgent and despatch them quickly. Post paid (sic) is delayed. I am deeply upset. Write at once.

March 28, 1853.

++ In 1850 Ghalib was imprisoned for gambling and debts.

To Har Gopal 'Tufta'

...Today the postman brought a letter from the Babu Sahib* with Mendhulal Kayasth 'Ghammaz's' application to the Maharajah... that Hardeo Singh had brought the *Diwans* of Janiji and of the Poet of Delhi⁺ for the Maharajah of Jaipur and was trying to get Janiji a job in the State... I had written to him to recall Hardeo Singh and not spoil his own chances because of me...

April 5, 1853

To 'Tufta'

...Janiji has written that the Raja was pleased with the *Diwan*. Janiji's man is waiting for the result. Rawalji has gone to receive the new agent.

(1853?)

To 'Tufta'

Bhai, I read in the *Zabdat-ul-Akhbar* that the Rani Sahiba has also died. Yesterday a friend wrote from Akbarabad (Agra) that both the Raja and the Rani are gone and nothing is settled about the State... Sahib, the Jaipur affair is now not worth considering. The new Raja is a frivolous youngster... And as for your information that the young Raja keeps reading my *Diwan* and never parts with it—well, you write this on the dubious authority of Munshi Hardeo Singh. How can I believe him? And also that according to the Babu Sahib, 500 rupees and a *khilat* have been decided for Mirza Sahib (Ghalib) and that he would bring it soon after Holi—Phagun, Chait, Baisakh—I don't know in which month Holi falls now? Earlier it used to be in Phagun!!

---
* Jani Bankey Lal 'Rind', a disciple of Ghalib.
+ Ghalib

Babu Sahib has sent two *hundvis* of a hundred each, one for Ahmad Hussain 'Mekash' for his writing the *tarikh** (date) of the Kunwar's birth and one on his own behalf as *nazar* for becoming my pupil...

1853.

To Har Gopal 'Tufta'

...One hundred rupees I had borrowed from Babu Sahib to pay the English merchant for that thing+ which is forbidden in my religion.....

June 9, 1853.

To Qazi Abdul Jamil 'Junoon' of Bareilly

...No mushairas are held in town. Inside the Fort a few princes get together and recite their verses. Once in a while I attend these gatherings. Contemporary society is about to vanish. Who knows when the poets would meet next or meet again at all.

1854.

To 'Tufta'++

...You ask me how I have continued to stay here. Well, I have lived in this *haveli* for the last ten years. In the neighbouring *havelis* live the hakims who are in the service of Raja

---
* Each letter of the alphabet has its numerical value. The date of birth, marriage and death, as well as of events of personal or national importance are calculated through the arrangement of letters in a word or phrase embodying the name, included in the final couplet of a quartrain or a poem. Personal names are also chosen in a way that indicates the date of birth.
+ Wine
++ This letter was written after the Munity. Other letters follow, describing the poet's plight and the destruction of Delhi.

Nardender Singh of Patiala. The Raja had taken a pledge from the English that these people would not be touched during the sack of Delhi. So, after the conquest, the Raja's sepoys came here to stay and the locality was saved. How else could I still be in the city? The rich and the poor alike have fled for their lives, the rest have been banished. I am afraid to write in detail. The employees of the Fort are suspects, are being questioned and punished, mainly those who served under the King during the Mutiny..... I am merely an impoverished poet who had been appointed to write the Mughal's history and to improve the King's poems. You may call it service or manual labour... I cannot stir out of my house. Who is there in town to visit? The homes are deserted and lampless. Martial law is in force since the 11th of May, Let's wait and see if the Muslims are allowed to resume living in Delhi...

December 5, 1857.

To 'Tufta'

...I did not run away, did not hide, was not questioned, did not go to meet officials, did not send them petitions. Haven't received my pension since May. Think how I must have managed.

January 3, 1858.

To Nawab Allauddin Khan 'Alai' of Loharu

    Each soldier of England is now a potentate,
    Men are mortally scared to go out in the bazaar,
    The Chowk is the execution ground, the houses dungeons.
    Each speck of Delhi's dust,
    Is thirsty for the Muslim blood.

You can't come across the town,
Or go from hence to the other side.
Ev'n if you meet your woeful friends—
Oft bitterly,
Oft a-weeping,
They describe their sorry lives and bruised hearts.
Can such meetings, Gracious Lord,
Erase the scar of separation's pain?

1858.

To Mirza Shahabuddin Ahmad 'Saqib' of Loharu

...Be just. How can I trace my looted goods? The loot has been sold off on the quiet. And even if it has been sold on the roadside how can I find out? Be patient. Bear the loss. Keep quiet.

Hope you have heard about the situation here. I'll tell you all if we remain alive and are destined to meet again. Otherwise, the story is over. I am afraid to write more.

February 8, 1858.

To 'Tufta'

...Why seek my permission to send me your poems? Do send them along although I am no longer a practising poet, like an aged wrestler can only teach the tricks of the trade. Don't think I am exaggerating. Can't write verse any more. I am amazed at my earlier work and wonder how I had composed all that.

April 12, 1858.

To 'Tufta'

...A friend of mine like you in sorrow.* He had adopted his nephew—a handsome Khatri youth—who died at the age of nineteen. The bereaved father has now asked me to write a *tarikh* as an elegy which he can recite and weep. Bhai, his request is precious to me, but I have a mental block and can't write poetry. You have faced the same tragedy and would be able to write the elegy with deep feeling. Write about thirty couplets in the form of *masnavi* incorporating the *madda-i-tarikh* in the final line. The boy's name was Brij Mohan and was affectionately called Babu.....

April, 1858.

To Mir Mehdi 'Majrooh'

Mir Mehdi, understand my situation. I have learned to live without eating. Don't worry about me. I spent the Ramzan 'eating' the fasts. God will provide in the future. And if I don't get anything else there is plenty of grief to sustain me.

May, 1858.

To 'Tufta'

...Still no letter from you. Once I was surrounded by friends all the time. Now among my friends only Shivji Ram Brahman, Balmukand Das and his son visit me often..... No news of friends in other cities..... How is Agra? Are people scared?

June 19, 1858.

---

* Tufta's son Pitamber Singh had died and on his death he had composed an elegy of 322 couplets.

To Mirza Hatim Ali Beg 'Mehr'

...In the prime of his life Major John Jacob got killed..... He is one of the thousands I am mourning ...How is Raja Balwant Singh?** Is he still getting the annual two thousand rupees from the English Government?

Ah, Lucknow. I still do not know what happened to that fairyland, what befell its men and women and what was the fate of the members of the House of Shujaudaulah!

1858.

To Mirza Hatim Ali Beg 'Mehr'

...I have never kept my poems with me. Nawab Ziauddin Khan and Nawab Hussain Mirza used to collect whatever I composed. Their houses were sacked, and their libraries destroyed. Now I yearn for my own poems. The other day a beggar, who has a good voice, got hold of a *ghazal* of mine from somewhere. When he showed me that piece of paper I wanted to cry.....

1858.

To 'Mehr'

...Among the poets, Firdausi; among the mystics, Hasan Basri; and among lovers, Majnun... they crown the lists in these fine arts. The pinnacle is reached when a poet becomes Firdausi, the faqir Hassan Basri and the lover Majnun... Laila had died before him. You have survived your beloved... The sons of the Mughals are incorrigible. When they love, they love with a vengeance and destroy the object of their

---

** Son of Raja Chet Singh of Banaras. Harassed by Warren Hastings, he had left Banaras and settled in Gwalior. An Urdu poet, the Raja was a friend of Ghalib and a disciple of 'Mehr', a nobleman of Lucknow.

passion. I, too, am the son of a Mughal, my ardent love proved fatal for a *femme fatale*. It happened over forty years ago, but still, with a pang, I remember her ravishing allure.

1859?

To Shiv Narain 'Aram'

Sahib... where are the men who would buy newspapers?* The traders and the mahajans who live here now go around looking for cheaper rates of wheat. If they are very generous they would give you the correct measure of grain, why should they spend money on mere paper?

1858.

To Mir Mehdi 'Majrooh'

...What nonsense you talk. How could I publish my books? Don't have enough to eat and to drink. Winter is coming and I have to worry about quilts and mattresses. Publish books indeed! Rai Ummid Singh of Indore had come to Delhi. He saw the manuscript and decided to get it printed. My beloved disciple Har Gopal (Tufta) was in Agra, and I sent the manuscript to him. The price was fixed at eight annas per copy. Fifty copies were bought (in advance) by Ummid Singh, who sent 25 rupees as *hundi* to the press and the printing began. Five hundred copies would be printed. Out of his fifty, Ummid Singh will probably give twenty-five to me which I'll distribute among my friends and relatives.

1858

---

* Rai Bahadur Shiv Narain 'Aram' belonged to Agra where he published an Urdu newspaper from his press. He also published Ghalib's books. His grandson Shri Mathur still lives in Agra and possesses some rare photographs and letters of Ghalib as family heirlooms.

To 'Tufta'

...Mirza Tufta, you can be cruel. You have no pity on the destruction of Delhi and seem to think that the city is still flourishing. Here one can't get hold of a *necha-band* (hookah-maker) leave alone calligraphists and artists. If the city was as of old I wouldn't have bothered you (to supervise the publication of the book). Please tell Munshi Shiv Narain not to print my Mughal titles. It will be harmful. Just print: 'Asadullah Khan Bahdur Ghalib'.

Sepetember 3, 1858.

To 'Tufta'

...The followers of Islam have been forbidden to live in the city. Their houses have been confiscated.

September 1858.

To Shiv Narain "Aram"

Beloved son. I did not know that you were Nazir Bansidhar's grandchild. Listen: In Nawab Najaf Khan's* time your great-grandfather and my maternal grandfather Khwaja Ghulam Hussain Khan were comrades and friends. When my grandfather left the service your grandfather too, discarded the sword, and did not work anywhere afterwards. In my youth your grandfather was manager of my grandfathers estate. We were the same age and very close friends. His house was not far from ours. I used to fly kites on the roof top and hold contests with Raja Balwan Singh... Our mansion in Agra has now been bought by Lakhmichand Seth...

October 19, 1858.

---

* The last of the powerful ministers of the Mughal Empire.

To Shiv Narain 'Aram'

...About the King's portrait this is a deserted city. The artists have lost their paintings and studios. One or two who have returned to town are now destitute. One of them has a miniature on ivory but demands thirty rupees for it, and says he sold these to Englishmen for three guineas each... I have asked some people to get you a picture on a reasonable price. I can't afford to buy one from this fellow and don't want you to waste your money.

October 23, 1858.

To Nawab Anwaruddaulah 'Shafaq' of Kadaura (Bundelkhand)

...As to your query about the comet, I wonder what to write. For there are no books here and no observatory... I have some acquaintance with the science of stars, otherwise have no other talent except a poetic turn of mind... Such stars appear in evil times. In Shajehanabad (Delhi), a comet was seen several evenings over the western side, after sunset. It created a sensation, but it hasn't been seen for the last twelve days. I only know that it means God's wrath and destruction of the country.

On the first of November, on Wednesday, the city was officially illuminated: The Company handed over India to the Queen. Governor-General Lord Canning Bahadur was appointed her regent in this land.

...Allah. Allah Allah.

November 5, 1858.

To Shiv Narayan 'Aram'

Mian, I was most happy to learn about your knowledge (of English). Yes, I will certainly take your help whenever I want anything written in English. Diwali is over. Send my books first before you set off on a pilgrimage to the Ganga.

November 9, 1858

To 'Tufta'

...General pardon has been announced, The fighters come one by one, surrender their weapons, and get the pardon.

November 20, 1858.

To 'Tufta'

...I feel sorry for Umrao singh but envy him too. Imagine! He has been free of his chains twice over, and here I have been carrying my noose for over half a century.....Tell him, "My dear fellow, I'll look after your children, why get into the trap?" ...You have spent the money in the bank. What would you do now? Mian, my advice and your understanding are both irrelevant. The Wheel continues to roll. Whatever has to happen, happens. One would act if there was free-will. One would say something if something could be said. Look, Mirza Abdul Qadir 'Bedil'* writes:

> What is fondness for glory, what contempt for the world,
> Follow or ignore the desires—even they would pass.

Look at me. I am neither free nor bound, neither afflicted nor in good health. Neither dead nor alive. Yet I go on living, keep on talking. Eat every day, drink occasionally. When

---

* Famous Persian poet of India.

death comes I shall die. I am neither grateful to God, nor do I complain. What I say is by way of a fable. Anyway, wherever and in whatever manner you live, write to me every week.

December 19, 1858.

To 'Mehr'

...Have a heart. There is plenty of 'French' and 'Champagne' in the Parsi shops here. The sahukars are rolling in money and jewels. What difference does it make to me?

December 20, 1858.

To Shiv Narain 'Aram'

Mian, what shall I write in Urdu (prose)?... Am I expected to go around for short stories and fables? I do not possess a single book. Once my pension is resumed I'll collect my wits. *Pet paren rotian, Sabhi gallan motian.*

(Punjabi: Once the stomach is full, everything looks fine.)

January 4, 1859.

To Mir Mehdi 'Majrooh'

...Mirza Jawan Bakht, Mirza Abbas Shah and Zeenat Mahal have reached Calcutta to go abroad. Lets see if they stay in Cape Town or proceed to London.

December 23, 1858.

To 'Tufta'

...In this loneliness my correspondence has kept me alive. When I receive a letter I feel as if its writer himself has graciously arrived..... The day is spent writing and replying letters.....

December 27, 1858

To Shiv Narain 'Aram'

... You want to publish my Urdu letters. But there is hardly a note which I have written carefully. This is casual writing and its publication would clash with the grandeur of my poetry. Apart from this, why should our personal correspondence be made public? No. I don't want my letters printed.

January 4, 1859.

To 'Tufta'

...Raja Ummid Singh came yesterday. Showed your letter to him. After reading it he said that he did not intend staying in any other temple, wanted to set up his own *takia* (Sufi faqir's abode). "My men have gone to Bindraban," he said, "to buy a house there. I'll live there in my religious manner. Write my salaams and also the message that (Tufta's) *Tazmin-i-Gulistan* as well as his *Diwan* has been sent to a Parsi in Bombay who will forward it to Tehran."

> Tufta, you've conquered India in your verse.
> Come, it's time to conquer Tabriz and Shiraz.

January 26, 1859.

To Mir Mehdi 'Majrooh'

Syed Sahib, listen. As if the English soldiers were not enough, the thanedar of Lahori Gate now sits on his stool by the roadside. Whoever gives the Tommies a slip and comes out is at once arrested : five lashes or two rupees fine. Tickets (sic) are being checked at every police station. The other day a jemadar came over to cross-question me. I said to him, please write down: "Asadullah Khan, pensioner, who has lived in the haveli of the Hakim of Patiala since 1850, never stirred out of his house either in the reign of the 'blacks' or of the 'whites' (during the Mutiny). Now his stay here depends on Col. Brown's orders." Then I sent this note to the kotwali. According to a rumour five thousand tickets have been printed; any Muslim who wants to live in Delhi must give a *nazarana* to the British officials and get the ticket to live within the city... *Almulk-i-lil-lah, walhukm-i-lil-lah* (The country belongs to God, the order is Gods!)

February 2, 1859.

To 'Tufta'

Received your letter last evening. For the address of a well-known person the name of the locality is not necessary. I am a poor man but letters come to me in Persian and English, occasionally with no name of the locality on the envelope. A few letters in English come from England... They would hardly care to know about a wretched place called the Ballimaran.....

February 19, 1859.

To Shiv Narain 'Aram'

...I am glad that *Dastambo** has been sold. Who bought the copies—Englishmen or Indians? Bhai, the light has gone out of India. The land is lampless. Lakhs have died and among the survivors hundreds are in jail. Those outside cannot afford to buy books. I think the English must have bought its copies and it must have been seen to Punjab. Fewer copies must have been sold in the Purab.

April 19, 1859.

To Mir Mehdi 'Majrooh'

Bhai, I have no paper and no stamps. I have taken off this page from a book, and am sending it to you in a used envelope. Do not grieve. Got some money last night, shall send for notepaper and envelopes today..... Something called 'pon tooti' (Town duty or octroi) has been levied on everything except grains and dung cakes. Large areas will be cleared around the Jama Masjid. Shops and houses will be demolished. Darul-baqa (a famous college of oriental Islamic learning) has been pulled down. Only God's name remains. Spades are active on either side.

November, 1859.

To Nawab Yusuf Mirza

...Helplessly I watch the wives and children of aristocrats actually begging from door to door. One must have a heart of steel to witness the contemporary scene.

November 28, 1859.

---

* Ghalib's account, in Persian, of the Mutiny

To Mir 'Majrooh'

What do you want to know and what shall I write? Delhi meant the Fort, the Chandni Chowk, the daily bazaar near the Jama Masjid, the weekly trip to the Jamuna bridge, the annual fair of the flower-sellers. These five things are no more. Where is Delhi now? Yes, there used to be a city by this name in the land of India.

December 2, 1859.

To 'Mehr'

...Nawab Governor-General Bahadur will arrive on December 15. Let's wait and see where he stays and how the durbar is held. In earlier durbars the seven jagirdars (of the seven states near Delhi) held their own courts. They were Jhajjar, Ballabhgarh, Farrukhnagar, Dojana, Pataudi, and Loharu. The first four States were wiped out during the Mutiny. Dojana and Loharu are now under the administration of Hansi-Hissar. Pataudi remains. If the commissioner of Hissar brings along the two nawabs, it would mean three. Of the general durbar the mahajans are all there. Among the Muslims (nobility) only three survive. Mustafa Khan in Delhi, Meerut; Maulvi Sadruddin in Sultanji (Nizamuddin), and in Ballimaran, Asad. All three condemned, doomed, despondent and grief-stricken.

> Once we broke beaker and glass,
> Let rosy wine rain from the sky.

December 2, 1859.

To 'Tufta'

...I find both Avicenna and Naziri to be futile. To live one's life one requires just a little happiness; philosophy, empires, poetry are all nonsense. If the Hindus had their avatars and the Muslims their Prophets, so what? If you lived as a famous man or as a non-entity, what of it? One should have some means of reasonable livelihood, and good health. The rest is all illusion... Soon this illusion may end too. My means of livelihood and my health may vanish and I may reach the state of void. In this silence in which I find myself now, I am not aware either of myself or this world or the hereafter. I duly answer questions, continue my dealings with others, but know that all this is a delusion, not a river, but a mirage, not life but vain glory. Both you and I are fairly good poets. Agreed that some day we might become renowned like Saadi and Hafiz. But what did they gain that we would?

1859.

To 'Tufta'

...My dear, how do you expect every one to become Tufta and Ghalib?... You say I have counted so and so among my relatives... Dearest friend, I consider all humanity to be my family; every man, be he a Muslim or a Hindu or a Christian, is my brother. Others may not accept this but it does not matter.

December 23, 1859.

To 'Majrooh'

Mir Mehdi, aren't you ashamed of yourself when you say in your couplet: 'Mian, this is the language of Delhi'. From Jama Masjid to Rajghat Gate all is a wasteland. If the debris was to be removed the place would look haunted..... And the people are still proud of Delhi's language! What a laugh. Where is Delhi? It is now a military camp.

Haven't heard from Alexander Heatherly*....

1860.

To 'Tufta'

Mirza Tufta, in my despair only you can make me laugh. What did you get out of *Tazmin-i-Gulistan* that now you want to publish *Sumbalistan*? Why must you waste money?

March 30, 1860.

To Chowdhry Abdul Ghafoor of Etah (UP)

...I was five when my father died, nine when I lost my uncle. In lieu of his estate I and my family were awarded ten thousand rupees a year by Nawab Ahmad Baksh Khan. He gave us only three thousand...my share being 750 rupees a year. I informed the English government. Both the Resident in Delhi and the Secretary to the Government in Calcutta agreed to get me my share. But the Resident was dismissed and the Secretary died. After a long time the King of Delhi granted me 50 rupees a month, and the Crown Prince 400 a year. The Prince died after two years. The King of Oudh, Wajidali Shah, gave me an annual five hundred for writing his eulogies; he didn't survive for more than two years. That is, he is alive but minus his kingdom. The kingdom of Delhi took longer to die and provided me with my bread and butter for seven years before it fell. Now if I go to the Nizam of Deccan, the person who recommends me would either die or be sacked, or his efforts would fail, and the Nizam would not give me a thing. Or even if he does, his kingdom would fall and his realm laid waste.....

1860.

---

* A fine Urdu poet whose French father was a friend of Ghalib. Heatherly whose pen names were 'Azad' and 'Alec', died at the age of thirty.

To Mirza Hatim Ali Beg 'Mehr'

Mirza Sahib, I don't like the way you go on. I am sixty-five now, have spent fifty years in this colourful world of temptations. In my youth a sage had told me: "There is absolutely no harm in enjoying life, but be a fly on rock-sugar, never one in honey." I strictly followed that advice! You should grieve over someone's death only if you mortal yourself... Be grateful for your freedom. When I visualise Paradise and think in case I am forgiven of my sins (in the hereafter) and granted celestial palace—complete with a houri—the residence there would be permanent and eternity would have to be spent with the good lady—the very idea terrifies me. Ha, the houri would become a pain in the neck—the infinite monotony, the everlasting boredom. The same old emerald mansion. The same branch of the heavenly tree. The same old houri...

1860.

To 'Tufta'

Received your letter from Meerut. Congratulations on the publication of *Sumbalistan*. May God look after your prestige. The greater part of life is already gone, some is left—that too should pass well. What did Urfi achieve through his *qasidas* that I should advertise mine? What did Saadi get out of his *Bostan* that you would out of your *Sumbalistan*?

Apart from Allah all is vague and non-existent. There is no poetry sans no poet, no ode and no ode-writer. Nothing exists except God.

January 20, 1861.

To 'Tufta'

...Never think that what people wrote in earlier ages was always right. Weren't fools born in those days too?

1861.

To 'Tufta'

Look here, Mirza Tufta, you wasted your money, your poetry and my corrections. What a terrible copy (sic). You would have realised the difference between your verse and its copy if you were here and had seen the moon-faced begums of the Red Fort wandering around in the streets in filthy clothes, ragged pyjamas, and broken shoes. *Sumbulistan* is a beautiful girl in shabby clothes.

April 19, 1861.

To 'Alai'

...Why wouldn't I be fond of you? But to meet me either you must come to Delhi or I must proceed to Loharu. You are unable to do so and so am I. You wouldn't accept this as an apology unless you understand as to who I am and what it is all about.

Listen. There are two worlds—the world of souls and the world of dust and water. He is Master of both. Although the general rule is that the sinners from this world are punished in the hereafter, it also happens, that a sinner from the world of souls is sent down here for punishment. Therefore, on Rajab 8, 1212 Hegira, I was sent here for prosecution. Stayed in the lock-up for thirteen years. On Rajab 7, 1225 I was awoken from penal servitude, my feet were chained, the city of Delhi decreed my prison and the writings of prose and poetry assigned as my hard labour. After many years I escaped and wandered in the cities of the east. But they caught me in Calcutta and hauled me back. When they saw that the prisoner was footloose they manacled my hands..... Last year I left my chains behind and carrying the manacles with me ran away once again..... Was arrested in Rampur and dragged back. Pledged to myself that never again would I try to flee. How could I, had no strength left. I don't know when the order of my Final Release comes.....

June, 1861.

To Mir Mehdi 'Majrooh'

Mir Mehdi.....

...My dear man, Urdu Bazaar is no more, where is Urdu?... Why ask about the epidemic? After the incredible massacres, loot and epidemic the Great Archer had to shoot this arrow too ...

The Oracle (Ghalib) had said ten years ago:

> All calamities have befallen, Ghalib,
> Only sudden death remains.

But dying in the general epidemic I considered below my dignity.

July, 1861.

To Nawab Anwaruddaulah 'Shafaque'

...I too have been persecuted by my relatives. Of the people of my own race a handful may be in Samarqand and a few hundred in the Dasht-i-Qapchaque (The Volga Basin). But here I do have many kinsmen and have suffered at their hands for sixty-one years.

October 22, 1861.

To Mirza Shahabuddin Ahmad Khan 'Saqib' of Loharu

...left for Hapur. My grandsons left earlier on horseback. Reached the serai at Hapur in the afternoon, found the boys and the horse already there... left at dawn, reached the serai at Babugadh by surprise. Spread a cot, put my bedding on it, and am now smoking the hookah. The extra horses have arrived, the boys are coming in the *rath*.....

(Probably 1861.)

To 'Alai'

Mian, I am in great distress. The walls of the *mahalsara* (ladies apartment) have collapsed, so has the bathroom. The ceilings are dripping incessantly. Your aunt feels she'll be buried alive any moment. The *diwankhana* (men's apartment) is worse. I am not afraid of dying but the lack of comforts unnerves me. The ceiling has turned into a sieve. If it rains for two hours, the ceiling trickles for four. The landlord can repair the house only when it stops raining. And how would I live here during the repairs? Could you lend me the *haveli* (in which Mir Hasan lived) for your aunt and the upper floor of the kothi (where the late Ilahi Baksh resided) for myself? After the rains and the repairs the Sahib and the Mem and the Baba-log would return to their old haunt.

July 28, 1862.

To Alauddin Ahmad Khan 'Alai'

It's raining hard. I'm sitting near the brazier; I write two lines and warm the note paper over the fire. Give my regards to

Bhai Sahib and tell him that the time has gone when I freely borrowed from Mathura Das, Durbari Mal, and Khub Chand Chainsukh, and merrily gave them I.O.Us. My mother, aunt and the Khan (The Nawab of Laharu) were there to look after me. Now I get just 62 Rupees from the Collectorate (family pension), and a hundred from Rampur. The fellow who lends me money wants his interest every month. Then the income tax, the chowkidar's pay, wife and children, servants...

July 28, 1862.

Maulana Alai: I do not fear death nor do I claim to have patience. It had rained hard, the younger boy was scared. His granny was also upset...... Now it has stopped raining. The boy and the wife are not afraid any more; I am not uncomfortable either. The open terrace, the moon, a cool breeze, Mars visible in the sky all night. In pre-dawn Venus glimmering. As the moon sets in the west, Venus appears in the east. The delight of a sip of wine, the glowing night.

August 6, 1862.

To Mir Mehdi 'Majrooh'

...In *Oudh Akhbar* saw the news of the King's death. Couldn't confirm it...

November 20, 1862.

To 'Tufta'

...What you say is unkind and is based on a misunderstanding. Good God, can I ever be cross with you? What can you write that I would mind?..... I had only one brother who remained mentally deranged for thirty years and died. Were he alive and sane and if he had spoken against you I would have scolded him. Bhai, nothing is left in me now. The miserable rains have receded but advancing age has become more wearisome. I lie in bed all day long. Can't sit up, often write lying down.

November 27, 1862.

To Mir Mehdi 'Majrooh'

...The Jama Masjid has been released from military custody. *Kababias* have set up a shop on its stairs; eggs, chicken and pigeons are being sold.

On Friday, November 7, 1862, Abulzafar Sirajuddin Bahadur Shah was released from the prisons of the British and of his mortal body. *Inna l'iLlahe wa Inne alha rajeoon.**

...I am sitting in the sun with Yusuf Khan and Lala Hira Singh. After giving the envelope to the man, shall go home where one verandah receives some light. Shall sit there, wash my hands, eat one *phulka* dipped in *salan*, wash my hands with *besan*, come out in the courtyard again. Then God alone knows who would turn up, which friends arrive, what sort of company I would have.

December 16, 1862.

To Mir Sarafaraz Hussain

...Your letter did to me what the smell of (Joseph's) cloak had done to Jacob. Mian, you and I may be old or young, strong or frail, we are precious, valuable beings. As some cynic has said:

> Monumental that we are,
>
> Forget us not for we are legends.

---

* From the Quran: From God we come and unto Him we return.

52

It is the same upper floor. I look at the staircase. That's Mir Mehdi coming, and Yusuf Mirza, and Meeran, and Yusuf Ali Khan. I am not mentioning those who are dead...Allah! Ali Khan. I am not mentioning those who are dead ... Allah! Allah! I am mourning thousands. When I die who is left to mourn for me?

1863?

To 'Alai'

...I have told you already that I do not remember the quatrains you want. And again you ask me to send them to you as though I have been lying. Bhai, I swear by the *Quran*, the *Gospels*, the *Torah*, the *Psalms*, the four *Vedas*, the *Zand*, *Pazand* and *Avesta*, and by the Guru's *Granth* that I do not have either that wretched ode or those quatrains with me.....

June 11, 1863.

To 'Alai'

I envy the Island-dwellers,* especially the Rais of Farrukhabad (Taffazul Hussain Khan) who was taken off the ship and left to wander on the soil of Arabia.

June 19, 1863.

To Mir 'Majrooh'

The rains, yes listen: First there was the Mutiny, the demolition of the houses, the epidemic, the famine. Now the downpour for the last 20 days. Once in a while the sun briefly glimmers like a flash lightning. If ever the stars come out at

---

* The rebels of 1857 who had been transported for life to the Andamans.

night, people take them to be fire-flies or glow-worms. In the pitch black nights the thieves have had a glorious time. Daily, one hears of burglaries. Thousands of houses have collapsed, killing hundreds. Lanes have turned into streams. In the *ann kaal* the drought killed the crops. This *pan kaal* has swept the sown and unsown seeds away.....

July 29, 1863.

To Har Gopal 'Tufta'

Your poetry has become very mature, does not need any improvement. The lion teaches his cub till a certain time, after which the cub grows up and does his own hunting.

(Perhaps 1863.)

To 'Tufta'

...Stop writing odes to the rich. Write love poetry and remain happy.

November 24, 1863.

Maulana Alai... perhaps five days back Munshi Naval Kishore* left for Lucknow by the Dak (mail-cart). He might have reached there yesterday or may reach today. When the Munshi Sahib and Shahabuddin Khan Sahib come here I said to the latter: had I been a worldly man, I would have called this employment, but since I am a faqir, I can say that I get sustenance from three sources: Rs 62 a month from the English Government, twelve hundred a year from Rampur, twenty-four rupees annually from the Maharaj here. That is,

---

* Munshi Naval Kishore, publisher of *Oudh Akhbar*, owner of the now legendary Naval Kishore Press of Lucknow.

he sends me a complimentary copy of his paper, four times a month and I send 48 stamps to his press.....

December 13, 1863.

To Qazi Abdul Jamil 'Junoon'

...The Family of Learning has been as much ravaged as India was after the Mutiny. The illiterate are ignorant, the learned indifferent.....

May 8, 1864.

To Khwaja Ghulam Hussain Khan 'Bekhabar'

...I am a faqir disguised as a worldly man. I am seventy years old and apart from the jostling crowd of commoners a cavalcade of seventy thousand men of consequence must have passed before my weary eyes.....

1864.

To Mirza Qurban Ali Beg Salik

...they say to give up hope in God downright *kufr* (lack of belief). But I happen to have lost all hope in His bounty and have become an absolute kafir. So now, according to Islamic faith, I have no hope of redemption and have thus lost this world as well as the next. But you do your best to remain a true Muslim, don't you lose trust in God.

Whatever happens to the mystic is good for his soul.

July 11, 1864.

To 'Tufta'

...You know it is not my own but a rented *haveli*. The downpour began in July. The upper-floor verandah, where I spend all my time, has not collapsed but its ceiling has become a sieve. Trays, wash basins, *ugaldans* have been placed all over the floor to receive the rain dripping through. Inkstand and books have been put away in the store room. The landlord is not interested in repairs. I have lived in Noah's Ark for three months.

October 14, 1864.

To 'Tufta'

...Mr Rattigan is writing a book on Indian poets. He sought my help. I've sent him some books and the names of 16 living poets ...(including Tufta)..... He must have written to you... the English translation of the couplets will not be included in the book.....

December 9, 1864.

To 'Tufta'

...I thought you were in the Mohalla of the Qanungoes in Sikandrabad, while you are in Lucknow, inside Raja Man Singh's *haveli*, in the office of the *Oudh Akhbar*, smoking away the *madaria hookah*, chatting with Munshi Naval Kishore... Give him my salaams. The paper hasn't arrived, although it is Monday...

February 12, 1865.

To Nawab Alauddin Khan 'Alai'

...I did not get the acclaim for my prose and poetry which it deserved. My poetry was composed for myself alone... I neither have the strength to pick up a staff and a mug and set out on my wanderings on foot nor can I afford to have my table spread for all humanity. How I wished that if not in the entire world, at least in the town where I lived none should go ragged or hungry... I who cannot bear to see others beg must go from door to door, seeking sustenance.

February 13, 1865.

To Hakim Ghulam Murtaza Khan of Patiala

...I have never bothered you about anything. Now I beg of you for kindness. Pandit Brij Narain comes to you with this letter. His elders held high positions in the Sarkar of Nawab Ahmad Baksh Khan of Loharu. He now comes to Patiala seeking employment. I swear upon my head that if you do your best to get him a job in keeping with his prestige I would think as if you had given me that position. I shall be infinitely grateful...

March 11, 1865.

To Nawab Aminuddin Khan of Loharu

...Alai Maulai, the Vakil* of Asadullah's** durbar, forced the faqir to write a *ghazal*. If you like it please ask the singer to render it in the high notes of Jhanjoti. If I remain alive, shall come in winter and hear it.

July 26, 1865.

To 'Tufta'

...I didn't come here to get acclaim, but to beg. I get my daily bread from the Sarkar (Rampur). The Nawab is generous

---

* Agent
** Ghalib

and bountiful. Whatever one is destined to receive, one gets here... Munshi Naval Kishore's application was presented (before the Nawab). Some grant to him on the occasion of his daughter's wedding is being proposed.

November 28, 1865.

To 'Tufta'

Mirza Tufta, your second letter[+] Nothing is hidden from you. Am waiting for a little futuh.[++] You will share it with me.

To 'Tufta'

... When I was alive, Pandit Badri Prashad of Karnal used to send me his poems for correction. After my 'death' I wrote to him to send his work to Munshi Har Gopal Tufta for correction... I am old, weak, poor, in debt, deaf, hoping for extinction.

(Perhaps 1866).

To 'Tufta'

...Got your very sorrowful letter in Rampur. Had no time to reply. Fell ill in Moradabad... Why do you want to give up your attire (renounce the world)? What wardrobes do you have anyway that you would give them up? By discarding your formal dress you cannot escape the prison of life. You'll still have to continue eating. Sorrows and hardships, woes and comforts—make them one. Try to go on living.

> Ghalib you'll have to bear the shock,
> The event is bad, but life is dear.

[+] Apparently Tufta, too, had fallen on bad days and had sought Ghalib's monetary help.

[++] Sum of money or food that the devotees send to their Sufi.

To Mirza Shamshad Ali Beg Khan 'Rizwan'

Mirza, because of growing weakness I can't easily write letters. I have not given up writing. Writing has given me up... Do not worry when you don't hear from me. When I die you'll hear the news...

August, 1866.

To Mir Habibullah 'Zoka' of Nellore

...I am a Seljuqi Turk. My grandfather came to India from Trans-Oxiana in the time of Shah Alam. It was a decaying empire and he was employed by Shah Alam only to command a cavalry unit of 50 and was given some land. In the political anarchy of the time he lost it all. My father Mirza Abdullah Beg Khan Bahadur served under Nawab Asafuddaulah in Lucknow, and was later employed by the Nizam of Deccan to command a cavalry unit of 300. There too he lost his job during a civil war. Worried, he went to Alwar and was employed by Rao Raja Bakhtawar Singh. He was killed there in a battle. The Marathas had appointed Nasrullah Beg, my uncle, the subedar of Agra. He brought me up. In 1803 in the time of General Lake the Subedari was turned into a commissioner's division; an Englishman came as commissioner. My uncle became the brigadier of a cavalry unit of 400..... He had, for life, a jagir with nearly one lakh and fifty thousand rupees annual income..... He suddenly died. The cavalry was disbanded and a grant was fixed in place of the lands..... Went to Calcutta in 1830 and requested the Nawab Governor to renew my pension. The details of my estate were verified in the records, and I was granted a *khilat* (court dress) and court jewellery... After the Mutiny, because of my association with Bahadur Shah, the *khilat* was withdrawn..... Now I have received an ordinary *khilat*. This is the *khilat* of my estate, and not given to me for any services rendered...

February 15, 1867.

To Miandad Khan 'Saiyyah'

...I wrote lying down but now even that is not possible, because my hands tremble and my eyesight is fading fast. It is unbearably hot. I sleep in the courtyard at night. Two men carry me into the verandah and dump me in a small, dark side-room. I spend the day lying in its dingy corner. In the evening I am again carried out and dumped on a cot...

June 11, 1867.

To Nawab Kalb-i-Ali Khan of Rampur

...They are saying in the city that Your Highness have sent five hundred rupees to the window of Mufti Sadruddin for his burial. This Faqir also hopes that his corpse would not lie without grave and shroud.

I have another humble request to make. I owe nearly twelve hundred rupees to my creditors and would like my debts to be paid off in my lifetime*.....

July 27, 1867.

To Miandad Khan 'Saiyyah'

...I do not have a secretary. When some friends turn up I dictate my replies. I am a guest in the world for a few more days. What do the newspapers know about my actual condition?..... Poems for correction and letters continue to pour in and I feel ashamed and miserable. I am old, an invalid, completely deaf, half blind, and bedridden.

---

* He was in debt for 800 rupees at the time of his death.

The Indian photographer who was my friend has left the city. An Englishman takes photographs. How can I have so much strength as to go downstairs, sit in the palanquin, go to his house, sit for an hour or two in the chair to get the photograph taken, and then come back alive...?

August 25, 1867.

To Munshi Hira Singh

The light of Ghalib's weary, unhappy eyes, Munshi Hira Singh—my prayers. Spend the winter in comfort and do not worry. Educate your son during the year. When he acquires some knowledge request the Deputy Commissioner for promotion. If you become a naib-tehsildar chances are that sooner or later you would be appointed Extra Assistant Commissioner also......

January 14, 1868.

To Bihari Lal 'Mushtaq'

Talented and virtuous, obedient to elders, Bihari lal 'Mushtaq': through the prayers of unhappy Ghalib may you have a long life, greater progress and prosperity. I am sorry to hear about your gracious father, Munshi Bhavan Lal's death. Although I did not know this traveller on the Way of Transience, the thought of your bereavement and loneliness grieved me much. May God forgive him his sins and give you peace.

February 26, 1868.

To Mirza Shahabuddin Ahmad Khan 'Saqib'

... Prayers from Faqir Asadullah. Agha Mohammad Shirazi arrived by the evening train, came to visit this faqir in his shrine... When you see him you would think your old Uncle

Ghalib has become young again and has come to attend the festival.

Give my salaams to Col. Alexander Skinner* when you meet him.

To Mirza Qurban Ali Beg 'Salik'

... I don't expect anything from God Almighty, why talk of His creatures? It's an impossible situation. I have turned my own spectator, am pleased with my grief and dishonour. Now I imagine myself to be somebody else. When I get a shock I say: Lo, Ghalib has been hit by another stone. He thought no end of himself as a peerless poet. Go ahead, deal with your creditor, dear fellow! The truth is, with the death of Ghalib a great agnostic and non-believer is gone. After their death kings are referred to as Paradise-dwellers. Since this fellow fancied himself to be the Monarch of Poesy I would call him the denizen of Inferno. Aha, Najmuddaulah Bahadur!— One creditor has grabbed your collar, the other is giving you hell and I ask you: Nawab Sahib, you happen to be a Seljuqi and a descendent of King Afrasiab, what's all this, eh? Say something man! But what can the shameless creature say? He took wine from the *kothi* (English shop), roses from the perfumer, cloth from the draper, mangoes from the fruitseller, money from the jeweller—and all on credit. Did he ever think how on earth he was going to pay for all this?

(Probably 1868)

To Mirza Baqar Ali Khan 'Kamil'

...Prayers from half-dead Ghalib. I was delighted to hear about your job (in Alwar). As the Maharaja (Raja Shivdhyan Singh of Alwar) has told you, you'll soon be promoted...

---

* The legendary Col. Skinner, founder of the famous cavalry known as Skinner's Horse.

Last month I sent to Alwar a copy of *Sabd-i-chin*, along with a letter, through Mir Taffazul Hussain Khan. This week, I received a long and extremely kind letter from Huzoor Maharao Raja Bahadur. You must have heard of it. Why didn't you write to me about it? Now I ask you, am I mentioned in the Durbar, and if so, how? What does the Huzoor (the Raja) graciously say?

December 7, 1868.

Part II

HIS POETRY

translated by

Qurratulain Hyder

*Enter my thoughts' temple of Somnath
and behold
the stirring forms
adorned
with the sacred threads.*

— *Ghalib*

POEMS
Translated from Persian

The Ideal Men

When they see their blistered feet,
The wayfarers know
They move on planes higher than the galaxies
They o'ershadow the Milky Way.

The visible they observe with deep insight,
Secret thoughts, hid in the heart
They calmly read on the brow.
On the page of life they find no flaw,[1]
Errors for them are Anqa's[2] wings.
They see on earth
What they perceived
In Pre-Existence.

Seek them as guides, for,
Hotly pursuing the Path,
They view it as the Desert's throbbing pulse.
Eventide they contemplate

---

1. The Prophet's saying : "There could not have been a better world than this".
2. Mythical bird, supposed to be extremely rare.

On the morn's fluttering banner,
And daylight in darkened scenes.
What Persia says
They hear from Khusro and Shirin's lips,
What befalls Araby
They know in Wamiq and Azra's tale.

When they find themselves alone at table,
A sip of water
Is a kiss of the sword,
Bread is broken glass in their throats.

For them the vermilion mark on the brow
Illumines the glorious Hindu scene,
Wine they know as the light of the Parsis' festive joy.
The Zorastrian's chant, the Brahmin's holy thread,
And the Cross,
They see as their own rosary
And robe and prayer mat.
This changing world of night and day,
This cavalcade they watch detached.
The non-existent they find existing.
The invisible they easily see.

But they forget these marvels.
When in the magic spectacle of the poetry
Of all ages and climes
They come across my magic—
The waves of my lyrics softly flowing
In the Stream of Eternal Life;
In my prose they read Christ's healing words,
And they cease to remember
That the world is an illusion,
When they hear my voice
Emerging out of this transience.

A Persian Ghazal

They heralded the day in the dark some night;
Blew out the candles,
Received their crest from the sun.
They brightened my face, closed my noxious lips,
Snatched my heart from me, but gave me insight.
Wrecking fire temples
They granted me the inner flame;
Smashed the idols
So that I bewail
Thro' the conch shell.
In lieu of the pearls they'd plucked
From the proud banners of Persia's kings,
They gave me a treasure-sprinkling quill.
Tiara and crown
They took away from the Turks
Of Afrasiab's royal line,
And bestow'd on my verse
The grandeur of the Kayanis' reign.

They deprived diadems of precious gems,
And bejewelled my mind.
Whatever they acquired, passed on to me.
Tho' from the Zoroastrian
They received wine as his *jaziya*
To me they served it in Ramazan
On a Friday eve....

To My Beloved

Come, let's alter the course of the heavens—
Let the roving wine-cup
Change our fates.
We shall sit in a corner
And open all doors,
Unafraid of the Kotwal
Though he comes to persecute us,
And heedless
Of the Monarch.
Should he send us presents
We shall not accept.
Should Moses speak to us
We shall not respond.
If Abraham arrives
We shall give no greeting.
We shall strew blossoms

And sprinkle attar-of-roses
Along avenues and pathways.
We'll get some wine
And fill the cup,
And put it between us.
We'll dismiss the saki,
Turn out friends and music-makers,
And kiss each other with an abandon
That'll make the stars quiver and blush.
We shall hold back the dawn,
And banish the heat of the day.
We'll deceive the world, pretending
That the night is not over
And tell the shepherd to go back with his flock.
We'll lynch the bandits
Who come to extort from the rose-bower
Its tribute of flowers,
And chase them out with their baskets bare.

Softly shall we ask the early birds
To return to their nests.
You and I, my love, are the devotees of Hyder!*
We can send the sun hurtling back to the East!

—from a Persian Ghazal

---

* Hazrat Ali, son-in-law of the Prophet and the greatest saint of Islam, who is believed to have once miraculously turned the sun back to the East.

Charagh-i-Dair
(Temple Lamps)

May Heaven keep
The grandeur of Banaras,
Arbour of bliss, meadow of joy,
For oft-returning souls
Their journey's end.
In this weary Temple-land of the world.
Safe from the whirlwind of Time,
Banaras is forever spring,
Where autumn turns
Into the touch of sandal
On fair foreheads,
Springtide wears the sacred thread
Of flower-waves,
And the splash of twilight
Is the crimson mark of Kashi's dust
On heaven's brow.
The Kaaba of Hind, this conch-blowers' dell!
Its icons and idols

Are made of the Light
That once flashed on Mount Sinai.
These radiant, idolatrous naiads
Set the pious Brahmins afire
When their faces glow
Like moving lamps
On Ganga's banks.
Morning and moonrise,
My Lady Kashi
Picks up the Ganga-mirror
To see her gracious beauty
Glimmer and shine.
Said I one night to a pristine seer
(Who knew the secrets of whirling Time),
"Sir, you well perceive,
That goodness and faith,
Fidelity and love
Have all departed from the sorry land.

Father and son are at each other's throat;
Brother fights brother. Unity
And Federation are undermined.
Despite these ominous signs
Why has not Doomsday come?
Why does not the Last Trumpet sound?
Who holds the reins of the Final Catastrophe?"
The hoary old man of lucent ken
Pointed towards Kashi and gently smiled.
"The Architect," he said, "is fond of this edifice
Because of which there is colour in Life; He
Would not like it to perish and fall."
Hearing this, the pride of Banaras
Soared to an eminence
Untouched by the wings of thought.

Abr-i-Guhar-Bar
(The Pearl-Showering Cloud)

I am angry, Lord,
Ask me not to account for my deeds,
For the desperate can be irreverent and rude.
Bitter as I am, why must I hide my shame
And refrain from uttering a few words,
Since, being Omniscient, You know,
Anyway, how I feel?
You know, Lord, I have never
Denied nor rejected You.
The sun or the fire I do not worship.
I am not a tyrant, nor a killer,
Nor have I exploited and robbed others,
I am often sad, drink drowns my sorrows.
For inebriety and outrage
Why not question a few kings:
Jamshed, Behram or Parvez?

Why ask me, who in order to buy a drink,
Must degrade myself
And go abegging?
I retain neither troubadour nor harem
No dancer whirls on a carpet before me.
My house does not resound with laughter and song.
You goad me on towards the tavern at night.
Comes morning and you demand my blood.
Yearning for the company of some lovely lady
Fond of good wine,
I merely confront the coarse tavern-keeper
Demanding payment.
In springtime I am gloomy for I am poor,
Indigence keeps the doors of my house ajar.
Roses and tulips flood the world
With scent and colour,
But I sit brooding in my small dark room,
The hem of my robe tied to a stone.
My moments of joy are like
The frenzied dance of a beheaded man,

And no true echo of my ardent desires.
What would You get out of my poor rags?
Look at my broken frame:
Bowing before the worthless,
My head is covered with dust.
Kissing the thresholds of the mighty,
My lips are bruised.

POEMS
translated from Urdu

POEMS
translated from Urdu

Ghazal

In my kiosk of deepest gloom
Despondent night
Darkly looms.
Daybreak's sign—the softly-sinking light—
Is blown out too; all is quiet.
No call of Love
Nor Beauty seen, there's long been peace
'Twixt ear and eye.
Vision now
Golden liquor for me,
Courage my wine-girl.
With insight
I am drunk
My fancy is a tavern with no turmoil.

O newcomers to the hall of desires
Beware! if you yearn for wanton joys,
Observe me if you've the discerning eye,
Hark, if you want a homily!

Saki, in her splendour, is foe
To reason and faith,
The songster at the lyre
Robs sense and poise.
By night you beheld this pleasure dome
Was the gardener's mantle, the florist's tray;
The saki gait, the tuneful lay
Were a feast for the eyes, heaven for the ears.
Come hither at morn : all passion spent—
No music, no laughter, no merriment.
Burnt out by sad partings at early dawn
A candle remained,
That, too, is gone.
From Heavens come down such themes to me,
Ghalib, the quill's rustle is the Angel's song.

Selected Couplets

For a flask of wine
I go about pawning
My robe of piety, my prayer mat,
And greet again the wind and rain.

Night falls, the scene opens
Of the stars a-glow
Like the formal parting
Of temple doors.

My silence buries a million hopes.
I am
The burnt-out lamp
In the mute graveyard
Of the poor.

Suffering killed my belief in the reality of things
Can I say this is a scar on my heart?

Dreaming, my thoughts had *affaires* with thee—
Awake, there was no gain nor loss.

Still I learn in the school of grief
The meaning of 'gone' and 'was'.

The winding sheet
Did cover my bareness's shame.
On earth in all garbs
I had tarnished life.

How explain the heat of Fancy's core
I thought of madness, the desert was scorched!
The rose's scent,
The heart's wild groan,
The smoke of the lamp,
Whoever left your revelry,
Was disarrayed.

For me how tiny the world,
And
This ant's egg—the sky!

The man who sits in shadow of her wall
Is the monarch of the land of Ind.

Like the flash of lightning, in their house of sorrow,
The Free mourn for a mere instant.

The card-player of thought shuffles the scenes,
We are the turning of the leaves
Of a picture-book.

He granted me the twin Worlds
And thought I was glad,
I, too, didn't like to haggle with Him!

Sunset clouds
Remind one how
The rose bower
Was all afire
When you were gone.

A few, stayed back at each stage-post.
What else could they do
If they didn't find the Way?

Corridors of thought
Light up with buds,
Fancy reels
In the flowing bowl.

Once I gave up the tavern it matters not
If it's monastery, academy or mosque.

Do add Hell to Elysian Fields, O Lord!
Let's have more fun in after-life.

I'll copy it down in my roll of deeds
You did write a word in the Beginning.

What you and I call the battered sky
Is the crumbling old shrine of the anchorite
Called Ghalib.

I know constant grief is fatal,
But the heart cannot help;
Were there no sorrowing for love
I would still weep for the world.

When there was naught, existed God,
If all turned Void, He'd still be there.
Doomed am I, for I *am*,
Whatever could be if I were not?

Smoke curls up as the candle dies.
The flame of love,
When I was gone,
Wore sombre weeds.

I would recall the vast number of
Blighted hopes.
Lord, you'd better not ask
To account for my deeds.

From slumbering Fate
I could purchase
A dream or two.
But how would I
Pay their price?

Admire me, too, O Lord!
For the desire of vices missed
If this be the punishment
Of my committed sins.

Not the flowering aria
Nor the string of lute
Am I
But the tone of mine own defeat.

Like a little combination lock
I was fated to part from you
At the moment of meaning.

Tempests of joy
Raise wave upon wave
Of flowers,
Of twilight
Of breezes,
Of wine.

The world did kill you, Asadullah Khan,
What happened to your zest, elan?

Where are they now?
(tho' some reappear as tulip and rose),
What faces hide beneath the dust!

Let streams of blood flow from mine eyes,
This lonely night,
I'll think they are tapers of amber light.

The sun teaches the dew how to fade.
I, too, am, till the Kindly Glance
Falls on me.

All pieces of Creation are in flux and decay,
The sun flickers as a lamp in the path of winds.

Here I sit and cry
For the vanished Town of Dreams,
The heart you dashed to bits
Was a many-splendoured prism.

Ghalib, keep the thread of Extinction well in view,
For it binds the stray leaves of Existence.

Unjustly caught on the Recording Angel's word
Was one of our men a witness, too,
    of what they wrote?

Thy claim of being Unique is just indeed.
No beauty with a mirror-like brow
Could dare confront and reflect Thee.

Eye-like under the eyebrow,
The tavern should be close by the arched mosque.

The Intoxicated inherit the Six Dimensions,
To the ignorant the world is all mundane.

Can the eye see the resplendent Beauty
Veiled in springtime?

Autumn, spring, all seasons
Are all alike for me, for my cage,
For the lament of my shorn wings.

Don't be lured, the universe
Is enmeshed in the net of Thought.

I am the air of Quest's Marvel Land,
My wail, its phoenix.

Disguised as a mendicant, Ghalib I watch
The doings of 'the generous ones.'

We've now fallen from grace, but yesterday
When an angel was rude to us you condemned him!

Carrying its reinless, unstirruped rider
The steed of years is galloping fast,
See where it stops.

If the Manifest and the Seeker and the Sought
Are one
What accounts for Knowing?

What's known as the Manifest is,
The Absence of the Absent,
They still dream who are not asleep.

Ghalib I have given up wine, of course,
But sometimes drink
On cloudy days and moonlit nights.

Kohl
Is the smoke of the fire
Of her eyes silent eloquence.

I had a thousand wishes
And each wish enough to stop the heart,
A hundred hopes fulfilled,
Yet, not enough, alas.

Ghazal

To me the world is children at play,
A passing show each night and day.

A triviality, Solomon's magic throne;
Mere trifles, the miracles we own.

May this be the last ocean of raging blood!
And yet I fear tomorrow's unknown flood.

Torn between true faith and the heretic view
I am pursued by the old, beckoned by the new.

Benumbed my hands but alive my eyes,
Leave the Cup and Wine before me awhile.

He is my friend, one with me in every way:
Why malign Ghalib in my presence, pray?

Selected Couplets

My friends
Could not cure
My frenzy ever;
In prison my thoughts
Had the vastness of deserts.

Quest complains
Of the heart's
Limitations,
The river's turbulence
Is lost
In the pearl.

If I had so much pain to bear
You should have given me several hearts...

Both rosary and sacred thread are frail,
The test of the Sheik-and-Brahmin lies
In the strength of their fidelities.

Seekers, I didn't wish
To be ridiculed
For my
Failure,
When I couldn't find Him
I lost my Self
And returned.

In my lonely sorrow
Do not invite me
To the rose-bower.
I cannot bear
The smiling
Flowers.

The sparrow is a handful of dust,
Caged nightingale a speck
Of colour.

The heart is gone
Or else
I'd have shown
You
My glowing wounds.
What shall I do
With this pageant of lights
When the lamp itself
Is burnt out?

I'm not scared of the Hangman,
Nor do I dispute the Preacher
In whatever guise He comes
I know.

Now let me away to a land
Where no one speaks my tongue,
Where no one sings with me.
To have a house with no walls,

No neighbour, no guard at the door;
With no one to care,
And if death should come,
No mourners there.

And yet I wrote of anguish
My verses dipped in blood
And for my pains
My hands
Were flayed.

The river of sins ran dry
And it but touched
The hem
Of my robe.

Why be scared of the lovers' cries,
Who is there to hear their plaint?

If the Tigris is not seen in the drop
And the fragment in the part,
It's child's play, not the
Inner Eye.

Merci, O Gale!
I do not yearn for wings
My dust flies in her lane!
All sense of time was lost,
Doomsday passed over me
As you left.

If there is none but Thee, O Lord,
Why this rondo, why this play?
Who are these fairy-faces, pray?
What is coquetry
And allure,
Why the waves
In fragrant hair?

What are kohl-edged eyes?
Whence this greenery
And the rose?
What are clouds,
Wither goes the wind?

It is so long since I was host
To mine own love;
It is long since my evenings
Were brightened by wine.
Afresh I crave to watch her on the balcony,
Her troubled hair about her face.
Again to have her face to face
Edged with collyrium her scimitar eyes.
To see again the belle of Spring

Lit-up, rosy and gay.
Prudence stifles me anew
For years I haven't in frenzy torn
My collar and cape to shreds.
O to retrieve those days and nights
Of leisure, to sit and muse,
And dream and dream of Love.

Odes to Ali

I

No speck of the glade
Is missed by the Spring.
The spotless tulips' shade
A mole on April's heart;
The mountain's shining blade
In drunken gale
A shattered jug of ale.

The leopard's spots
Goblets of jade
And orange-fresh the
Sparks of fire.

Clouds gather
The world in their arms,
Regrets go
A-picking flowers.

Bulbuls sing
O'er hill and dale.
Sleeping paths
Awakened by
The roses' smile.

If you wish to gather
The buds of May
In the tavern today,
Forget your glass in a niche of grass.
Have you lost your turban in a public house?
Go, seek it as a wave of scent
In flower-land.

If the Maniches of Thought
Paints the scene,
The lines of his compass
Would sprout verdant and gay
Like a youthful face.

The vale's grass-parrot
Its ruby-beak
Opens in a song for the Shah.[1]

Bent as a labourer is the sky
Which built his house
Whose bricks were moulded in Gabriel's eyes.
Heavenly Grace like the mason's string
Tapes its walls.
The nine spheres its ramparts and towers
The courage of the sufis its soaring height.

The Desert of Najaf[2]
The pride of the seers,
Its dust, the pilgrims' robe of Hope.

O Lamp of happy, summer nights
Who turns the moths into fireworks,
Who makes the bulbul
Blaze like a pomegranate bud,

---
[1] *Hazrat Ali*
[2] *Hazrat Ali's tomb in Iraq*

The house of mirrors[3]
Flies, peacock-like,
To get your glimpse…

For your sons[4] the crescent moon
Weeps and sheds star-tears.
From eye to heart Asad, a mirror of love,
His words revel in significance.
For, *your* wine reveals all secrets.

---

[3] *Eyes*
[4] *Hasan and Hussain*

II

The world is a pageant of the Beloved's Oneness:
We couldn't be
If the Beauty
Weren't self-contemplating.

I lived life with no joy,
Drew no morals;
The hopelessness of hope
Gave me this world nor the next.

Futile the disputes
Ov'r the melody of Being and Non-Being,
Of Reason and Craze.
The seekers meditate
To get some praise.
The conceit of learning,
Devotion and faith,

Worldly life and the austere state
Are all the last drops in the wine-glass of Forgetfulness.

Submission and acceptance—
Like loyalty and love—
Go about bewildered.
Grave-faced Knowledge,
Serene Intellect
Are trodden footprints.
Love wanders witless, bereft of the senses
Happiness is a petina over the wishing glass.
The rock-hewer* starves in his rival's fort,
The Besutoon reflects Shirin's sleep.

Has the son of man seen
The Righteous's breath igniting fires?
Who ever found a response for the heart's cries?
I hear the vast rhapsody of the world at large,
But bound,
Can neither praise nor denounce.

---

*Farhad.

For shame, what unsavoury nonsense I write.
Say 'Ali' and the doubts are gone.
Ali, the Manifest of the Creator's Grace,
The Apostle's love, the darling of Ingenuity's Realm
The dust upon which he walks
Turns into a hemisphere.
His doorstep's mirror
Glimmering with Gabriel's prostrations.

O Asadullah, Lion of God, this Asad[1]
Is a commodity in the market of sins.
None but you would buy him.

Trusting in your grace
He's become impudent in his demands,
Grant him a heart brimful of love, of Inner Peace,
And an eye that adores the Truth.

---

[1] *Ghalib*